GW00470456

HUMAN
DEVELOPMENT
A psychological and
spiritual journey.

Dr Patricia Sherwood

© 2015 Dr Patricia Sherwood

All rights reserved.

No part of the book may be transmitted or reproduced by any form or means, either me-
chanical or electronic, including recording and photocopying, or by any known storage
and retrieval system, without the written consent of the author, except in the case of short
quotations being used in a review

This book is designed to provide information and motivation to readers and is not intended as a substitute for the medical advice of physicians, a professional mental health
counsellor, or to provide professional psychological services to you. If you need expert
professional assistance, you should seek the services of a competent mental health professional. Neither the publisher nor the individual author shall be responsible or liable for
any person or entity with respect to any loss or damage caused, or alleged to have been
caused, directly or indirectly, by the information contained in this book. The publisher
nor author shall be responsible for physical, psychological, emotional, financial, or com-
mercial damages, including, but not limited to, special, incidental, consequential or other
damages. Our views and rights are the same: You are responsible for your own choices,
actions, and results.

All casestudies in this book are composites and do not relate to any one person.

National Library of Australia Cataloguing-in-Publication entry

Author: Sherwood, Patricia, author

Title: Human Development: A Psychological & Spiritual Journey /Dr Patricia Sherwood
ISBN: 9780980404432 (paperback)
Subjects: Life cycle, Human
          Change (Psychology)
          Developmental biology
          Developmental psychology
          Future life

Dewey Number: 155

Author Contact Details:
Dr Patricia Sherwood
info@sophiacollege.com

Dedication

To my children, Tara, David and Elizabeth, who first taught me the meaning of the early phases of life.

To my parents, Laurie and Lucy Dowling, who taught me the meaning of the later phases of life.

To my peers who, like myself, have learned the meaning of being sandwiched in the middle of the lifespan between the young and the old, the beautiful and the wise.

Acknowledgements

Why, why why??? is this happening to me at this age and what can I do about it? What direction should I take in my life at this time? These are the perennial questions of so many of my students and clients. They have inspired me to write this book. It is a shorthand answer.

I wish to honour all people everywhere who live through the challenges of life with courage and tenacity, with enduring qualities of grit, grace, gumption and guts despite not having a plan as to what to expect at each age, what is normal development and what is exceptional.

I especially want to thank Liz and Jenny for their remarkable passion and love for conveying to students in their teaching the beauty, depth and breadth of the life span with all its different ages and challenges.

Contents

We shall not cease from exploration
And the end of all our exploring
Will be to arrive where we started
And know the place for the first time.

—TS Eliott

CHAPTER 1

Your Age: Patterns, problems and opportunities

Introduction

Most of us at some time have asked: Does life have a road map? A plan that can give us advanced warning of the potholes in the road we travel called life. We can transform the old adage "life is lived forward and understood backward" into "life is understood and lived forward" so that we do not live to regret lost opportunities. This book aims to do just that, to reveal patterns that characterise different ages of our life and to present advanced knowledge and options for managing them. Certainly, we are individuals but nonetheless we are united by common patterns at the same age. Shakespeare (n.d, p230) brilliantly and ironically portrayed the different ages as like an actor playing different parts:

All the world's a stage
And all the men and women merely players;
They have their exits and their entrances;
And one man in his time plays many parts.
His acts being seven ages. At first the infant,
Mewling and puking in his nurse's arms
And then the whining schoolboy with his satchel,
And shining morning face, creeping like a snail
Unwillingly to school. And then the lover,
Sighing like a furnace…then a soldier
Full of strange oath…and then the Justice…
With eyes severe and beard of formal cut…the sixth age shifts
Into the lean and slipper'ed pantaloon,
With spectacles on nose…last scene of all,
That ends this strange eventful history

Is second childishness...
Sans teeth, sans eyes, sans taste, sans everything.

Shakespeare is referring to the inevitability of the progression through the different ages so that we realise nothing is permanent and we are ultimately all human beings sharing the same physical path of development as we age. However, there are within this framework, diverse physical, psychological and spiritual choices we can make along the way as we are confronted with life's issues. This is why some old people have smiling eyes and other old people look bitter and miserable. This book aims to reveal the secrets of ageing with smiling eyes and a content heart...not because our lives are without challenges and difficulties, but because we know what core choices we need to make to engender happiness as we move from one phase of our life to the next.

Happiness is achieved not by what material goods we have accumulated during our life; it is achieved by the skilful resolution of the core physical and psycho-spiritual tasks over our life span that determine the quality of our human relationships. I use the term psycho-spiritual development to embrace the emotional, social and individual development of the person who is driven to become fully who he or she is capable of being in the world. In Maslow's terms, such an individual is fully functioning and self-actualised, so they are able to maximise their own and others' happiness through their decisions. Self-actualisation is...

> the movement with increasing maturity from neurotic pseudo problems to the real, unavoidable, existential problems inherent in the nature of man living in a particular kind of world... Even though he is not neurotic, he may be troubled by real, desirable and necessary guilt rather than neurotic guilt...there is a good correlation between subjective delight in the experience, impulse to the experience, or wish for it, and basic need for the experience. Only such people uniformly yearn for what is good for them and for others and they are able wholeheartedly to enjoy it and approve of it (Maslow,1959, p.129).

Age related life patterns

7-year patterns

The Greeks, of whom Hippocrates was the most eminent, determined that the human life path is divided into 10 seven-year periods each with their own challenges and unique characteristics that affect people. Bryant (1993, p.51) argued that the seven-year span is the rhythm between the psychological or sensory soul experiences and the maturing of a human spirit over the years of the life span and he describes it as:

The acquisition and digestion of life experience. It modulates the rapport between the growing mind and the deeper unconscious levels of our being.

This traditional seven-year patterning of human psycho-spiritual growth has dominated Western thought and laid the foundation for many writers including, Watering, Lievegoed and Steiner. These seven-year periods each with their own unique challenges–physical, psychological and spiritual–represent the phases through which one becomes a fully functioning human being. The challenges of each seven-year phase are universal, although the approach to transforming them and integrating the challenges during these phases of growth, is influenced profoundly by culture and the individual's temperament and character. If one successfully meets these developmental challenges, life bears fruits of contentment, happiness and fulfilment. If one fails to navigate these developmental challenges, especially over several phases of development, there is a great likelihood that one will experience frustration, lack of fulfilment and discontent. As a person ages this congeals into bitterness at lost opportunities and regret at a life not lived as the best of the spirit of the person would have intended it. These seven-year phases are as follows:

Babyhood and early childhood: **0-7 years**
Childhood: **7-14 years.**
Adolescence: **14-21 years**
Young adulthood: **21-28 years**
Adulthood: **28-35 years**
Reflective adulthood: **35-42 years**
Middle age: **42-49 years**
Mature adulthood: **49-56 years**
Senior adulthood: **56-63 years**
Wisdom adulthood: **63-70 years**
Old age: **70-77 years**
Older age: **77-84 years**
Oldest age: **84 years onward**

Although some writers, such as Bühler and Rumke, follow the Roman division of five phases in the life span (Lievegoed, 2008), I have chosen to work with the 12, seven-year phases. They have been more widely used to provide a cogent structure for identifying the core tasks of being a human at different ages, and traditionally they have been used in most Western cultures to explore the rhythm that marks the key transformations in consciousness throughout the lifespan. Martin Luther (Bryant, 1993, p51) summarised:

The seventh year always transforms man. It brings about a new life, a new character and a different state.

Individual, cultural and family differences may profoundly influence how these developmental tasks are expressed and worked with, but these tasks remain core to all human beings and their peer cohort. In particular, the development of the human consciousness and the human spirit defined as deep connectedness with our essence, and through deep understanding of that essence, with other human beings is the core process of lifespan development. It is at the heart of most age related challenges, however differently presented at different ages and in different cultures. Wheeler, Ampadu, Wangari, (2002,p.71) see the development of the spirit of a person in community as the core feature of black African life span development expressed so profoundly by the phrase: "I am because we are." In contrast, Western life-span theorists often emphasize physical and cognitive developmental tasks at the neglect of the spiritual dimensions. I plan to provide a holistic model that incorporates the lifespan tasks of body, mind and spirit, based primarily on the anthroposophical model of human development.

The meaning of the word spirit in the context of this book, does not mean something otherworldly, or something that is religious, but rather it is the essence of our highest human potential that needs to be manifest in our lives for us to feel happy, fulfilled and truly powerful in our humanity. To illustrate by using an analogy, Qantas has Spirit of Australia scrawled across its planes. This does not mean that they are religious planes, or planes flying to another world. Rather it means that Qantas planes represent the essence of the best of Australia, its unique beauty, strength, innovation and expansiveness. A journey with Qantas at its best, should give one the experience of the spirit of Australia.

A time to be born, a time to die, a time to grow...

"I just run out of energy these days..."We hear this statement so often today. How seriously should we take it? Should we be alarmed by this feeling of exhaustion in the face of life's challenges, or is it just normal? This bodily experience is typical of the questions that age related patterns answer for us. The answer lies in the overall pattern of our lives, which constitute three basic phases described by Lievegoed (2008, p31) as:

1. A phase of *growth and development* both in height, width and weight that roughly represents from 0-21 years during which our energy levels are high and energy outputs are exceedingly active.
2. A phase of *equilibrium* from approximately 21-42 years, which represents a period in which our energy output is more than adequate for the demands of our lives. Even during this phase, we can still party most

of the night and go to work the next day. We can stretch our energy to cover most of the opportunities that arise.

3. A phase of *involution* during which our physical energy starts to decline and we find ourselves increasingly needing to do less and less and to ensure that we have adequate sleep and rest in our lives. This period starts around 42 years. It is normal during this phase to feel that one must conserve one's energy and that one can run out of energy if one overcommits, parties too hard or too long, or taxes oneself with extra burdens. This is the phase in which two jobs, two kids, two cars and two mortgages become overwhelming.

Lievegoed (2003, p.38) represents these phases graphically below and the associated psychological and development stages of the human spirit.

Psychologically, the first phase (0-21) is one of the child being open and vulnerable to the world of their family, learning from those around them and initially being immersed in the creative and imaginative experiences of the child's world. In adolescence, the psychological receptiveness arises from becoming immersed in the realities of the outer sensory world, realities that are often hostile and unfriendly but which must be integrated into the adolescent's experience of life. It is a steep learning curve because during this early

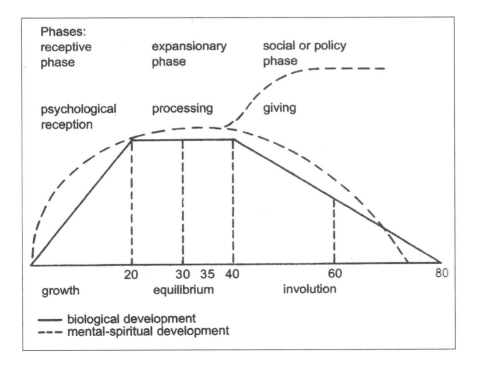

phase of development, the exposure to new elements and experiences is ongoing and often unrelenting, especially in our fast changing world.

Psychologically, the second phase (21-42) represents the vital processing of and creation of experience in the world and our mental energy is at its peak during this phase of the development. It is the peak phase for active engagement in the world, a phase in which we achieve our peak performances in the workplace and in our lives. During this expansionary phase, we acquire families, houses and careers.

Psychologically, the third phase from 42 years onwards marks declining mental and physical energy for work, careers and family. It can become a time of crisis for many who sense that their power in the world is declining. They feel uneasy because they have only measured their self-worth in terms of their performance in the external world. To transit this time with strength and happiness we need to become aware of what we can give to others, of the leadership we can provide from our experience (Lievegoed, 2003, p37).

In terms of the development of our human spirit, the 40s mark a critical point in our development. If we have not consciously developed our spirit through realising inwardly our potential, our gifts and our capacity to contribute to the wellbeing of others, then we are likely to find happiness elusive. We may seek it through endless cruises, travels, internet dating and anything else we can find to distract us from the reality of our physical decline that follows the 40s. Those of us who have worked to develop our humanity, who are in touch with the inner potential of our spirit are able – even in the face of physical and cognitive decline– to reach out to give. Through leadership in a range of work situations, we provide wisdom distilled from our previous experience. Lievegoed's diagram above graphically represents this successful transition to older age as the phase of giving, of social or policy leadership rather than contraction and collapse.

Human beings are an intricate combination of biology, psychology and spirit but it appears that the first three seven-year life patterns are largely biologically determined, the middle three life patterns largely psychologically determined, and in later years life patterns are predominately determined by our spirit. As our physical and cognitive capacities decline, our wisdom should flourish due to our lifelong experience and the maturing of the faculties of perception and insight.

Seven-year phases in patterns of three

The seven-year phases in patterns of three times seven-year phases throughout the lifespan act as a marker for the major transition periods in the human life. The first three seven-year period from birth to 21 years,

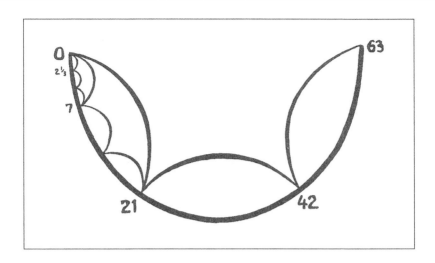

represents the phase that primarily is dedicated to bringing the physical body to maturity. Biology fundamentally dominates the developmental processes. From 21-42 years of age, it is the psycho-cognitive and emotional development that dominates the development process as persons have mastered their physical body and now exert their mental capacities and their feelings in shaping the world, sustained by a high level of physical energy. This three times seven-year phase from 21-42 years, is the peak performance period in terms of engagement in worldly activities. The three times seven period from 42 to 63 years, represents a decline in the physical body's strength and a lessening of cognitive performance. However, there is a great deepening of the psycho-spiritual development of a human being that occurs because of experience and reflection to create deep insight and wisdom. The 63-84 and 84 onwards phases continue the trends of the 42 to 63-year-old phase with declining physical and cognitive capacity, but an increasing ability to develop insight, wisdom and reflective intelligence.

These three times seven-year phases are diagrammatically represented above together with the three cycles within each seven-year period of development, which are influenced by the moon's rhythms (O'Neil &O'Neil, 1998, p.219).

Planetary influences: The seven-year periods and the development of different types of psycho-spiritual faculties.

O'Neil & O'Neil (1998, p.228) represent diagrammatically the planetary influences on particular seven-year phases of the life span. As the plan-

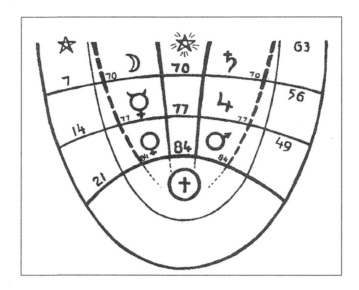

etary rhythms influence the rhythms of the Earth, so too they influence the rhythms of human development.

Moon: Babyhood and early childhood: 0-7 years

The Moon forces of babyhood provide the roundness, the beautiful serene glow that surrounds mother and infant and the magical moods of infancy where inanimate objects are as real as human beings and the world of make-believe is a profound psychological reality. The moon's fluidic influences in this period of development also enable the child to reshape the inherited physical body to one that better suits their life purpose (O'Neil & O'Neil, 1998,p.109).

Mercury: Childhood: 7-14 years

Mercury gives the child robust health, vaste amounts of energy and a zeal for life and learning as well as providing influences that bring wonderful creative and imaginative intelligence to bear on life. Here, the creative and imaginative powers of childhood lay the foundation for the adult cognitive qualities of innovation and problem solving. Children whose creative and imaginative play and learning is repressed by accelerated rational logical learning during this time will suffer in adulthood. They are most often afflicted by a brittleness in their thinking that results in uncreative thinking, weakness in innovative thought and problem solving. They may be good followers of set routines, but will be challenged by leadership positions that demand innovative thought and problem solving.

Venus: Adolescence: 14-21 years

Venus brings the attraction of romance, passionate love and the unleashing of the new forces of sexuality in the adolescent's consciousness. There is often an Aphrodite or Adonis-like beauty that shines from the adolescent during this period (O'Neil &O'Neil, 1998,p.109). It is a time when romantic love is born in the heart of a human being and the beginnings of a sense of sensual love dominates the psyche.

Sun: Young adulthood: 21-28 years; Adulthood: 28-35 years; Reflective adulthood: 35-42 years

The sun represents the power of life to create, nurture and sustain. Initiative and responsibility ripen and creative deeds in the world are implemented as life is at its zenith of human biological and cognitive potential. The sun's influence promotes mature experiential understanding and learning through insight in this period. The sun brings forth the energies that produce intellectual flourishing and growth of the human soul or psyche.

Mars: Middle age: 42-49 years

Mars promotes focused, concentrated consciousness and the urgency to fulfill one's destiny in the world. Mars imparts the energy to the individual to fulfill their potential and their life's destiny. It challenges the individual to rise above their culture and the norms of what is acceptable to achieve their highest potential even when this means stepping outside of the box.

Jupiter: Mature adulthood: 49-56 years

Jupiter promotes expansion of consciousness, awareness of one's deeper values and encourages the development of deep reflections and insight on life's experience. One's career must now be anchored more deeply in a meaningful framework or otherwise it becomes routine, dull and unsatisfying.

Saturn: Senior adulthood: 56-63 years

The influence of Saturn forces us into the narrow psycho-spiritual space where we must focus on the essence, or essential important features, of life that gives fulfillment and happiness. There is no room for distractions or diversions. We must sift through the chaff of our activities in the world to find the grain. We must focus only on the grain. The focus is the development of insightful wisdom about our own lives. Our activities in the world should be restricted to those things which are our unique gifts in the world.

All of the planetary systems above: Wisdom adulthood: 63-70 years; Old age: 70-77 years, Older age 84 years onward

All the planetary systems of the preceding years culminate in the wisdom of the aged, the "ego integrity" that Erik Erikson defines as the goal of our lives. If our spirit has successfully manifested its purpose and gifts in the world, we reap the fruits of this endeavour in this phase of the life span. We become content with who we are and we provide spiritual leadership and guidance from the fruits of the wisdom we have garnered throughout the phases of our life span.

In essence, it is important to remember that we are not alone, all parts of us are interconnected. We are energetically connected to each other, the Earth and the universe in which we live. There is a striking correspondence between the life rhythms within us as human beings and the rhythms of the world around us. We breathe on average, for example, 18 times per minute which is 25,920 times per day and this is identical to the Platonic Year, or passage of the sun's vernal point through the zodiac which is 25,920 years (O'Neil & O'Neil, 1998,p.179). The patterning of our age related experiences is directly connected to macrocosmic patterns of the movements of the sun, moon and other planetary systems throughout our universe. We are the microcosm of macrocosmic patternings which emerge during our lifetimes. The key to happiness and a fulfilled life is to know which patterns are emerging at which ages and what opportunities they present to us. It is the difference between swimming against the tide or swimming with the tide of our life's opportunities.

Model of the purpose of a human being's growth and development:
The fourfold model.

Many different models exist to explain the purpose of life span development phases. Freud posits a model that focuses on sexuality as the primary underlying process. Erikson focuses on the socio-emotional transitions and the tensions in different phases of development beginning with the trust versus mistrust struggle of babyhood and ending with the ego integrity versus despair of old age. Piaget focuses on cognitive development stages and Bandura on social learning stages. Kohlberg focuses on moral development stages throughout the lifespan. Bühler focuses on core life goals including need satisfaction, creative expansion, inner harmony and self-fulfillment (Peterson, 2010). While I will use elements of Piaget and Erikson in my analysis, my primary model will be the anthroposophical model of a human being developed by Rudolph Steiner, and upon which Waldorf schools base their education system, and anthroposphical medical practioners, nurses and therapists base their hospitals and patient care. This model is well documented in Therkleson (2007). It is termed the fourfold model of a human being, and its fundamental assumption is that the purpose of a human life

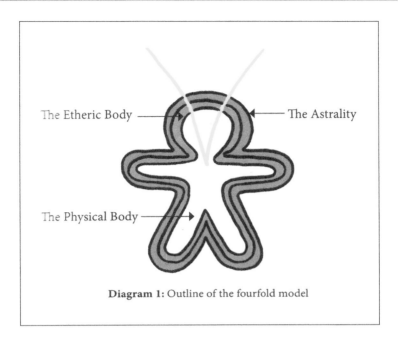

The Etheric Body ————→   ←———— The Astrality

The Physical Body ————→

Diagram 1: Outline of the fourfold model

is to manifest their unique spirit which carries the essence of themselves and which is termed the "I" in the physical world. To accomplish this it is necessary for their "I" to enter fully into the physical body which takes a complete developmental period of 28 years.

This is diagramatically represented above by Sherwood (2010, p. 24)

The etheric or chi force is the energetic layer interpenetrating the physical body that holds the life patterns of rhythm, which includes controlling the breathing, reproductive, digestive and circulatory rhythms of the body. It is the focus of Eastern medicine and is termed the chi force or pranic force. It is also known as the life force for it determines the vitality of a human being. Through the chakras it mediates the energy acquired in sleeping to the physical body and organs. If it is vibrant because it is well nourished and rested, the physical body will be vibrant. The etheric force provides a buffer between the physical body and the emotional and mental stressors of the thinking/feeling life which Steiner terms the astral. In contrast, the astral body– also understood as the "trauma system" or as the ordinary day-to-day mind– stores all the experiences, both positive and negative. It can also be termed the soul, as it connects the individual to the sensory world.

The "I" is the source of strength in an individual. It is that part of a person that can transcend difficulties and provide insight, understanding and courage. It has the capacity to connect and to transcend human limitations. It can connect to the highest sources of universal light, strength and power however these are named and expressed by the individual. It is the highest energetic vibration in the human constitution and the physical body is the lowest energetic vibration. In order for this higher spirit to connect into the body, it must come through the soul or astral body, which comprises day-to-day thinking and feeling often driven by our likes and dislikes, our fear and our joy. It is the realm of sensory experience, which is not always pleasant.

The "I" is the storage of memory and when we do not remember things, then our "I" is not fully in our body and we are dissociated from our bodily experience which can be described as "excarnated", or more commonly known as dissociated. When one is excarnated or dissociated one lacks mindfulness, and it is impossible to manifest the power of one's spirit in the world because one is not present to the physical world (Steiner cited in McDermott, 1984). At this point the thinking/feeling soul life, or astral, takes over with all its reactions and history of trauma, and runs the life in unskilful ways. The challenge of being a human being is to keep the "I" in the body so that the person makes skilful choices and is mindful in each moment of the life.

This process if hindered, results in a range of dysfunctional behaviours. Sherwood (2007) documents techniques and strategies for working with these arrested behaviour patterns in Holistic Counselling. It focuses on how the human being brings their "I" or spirit into their life and the opportunities and challenges to this process at different ages. It provides strategies to maximise one's potential and to strengthen the "I" to be present in the physical body and the individual's life.

It was Alexander Pope who so brilliantly described the challenges of being human when he described us as: "Created half to rise and half to fall, the glory, jest and riddle of the world."

REFERENCES

Bryant, W (1993) *The Veiled pulse of time: Life cycles and destiny* NY, Lindisfarne.

Maslow, A (1959) *New knowledge in human values*, Indiana, Gateway.

Lievegoed, B (2003) *Phases: the spiritual rhythms in Adult Life*. London, Sophia books.

Mc Dermott, R (1984) *The Essential Steiner*. New York, Rudolf Steiner press.

O'Neil, G & O'Neil, G (1998) *The Human Life* NY, Mercury Press.

Shakespeare (n.d.) *The complete works of William Shakespeare*. London, Abbey library.

Sherwood, P. (2007, reprint: 2010) *Holistic Counselling: A new vision for mental health* Bunbury, Sophia Publications

Wheeler, E., Ampadu, L, Wangari, E., (2002) Life-span development revisited: African centred spirituality throughout the life cycle *Journal of adult development*, 9(1), 71-78.

Trailing clouds of glory do we come
from God who is our home:
Heaven lies about us in our infancy ...

W. Wordsworth Intimations of Immortality from recollections of early childhood

CHAPTER 2

Living in the golden haze: 0-7 years

Introduction

Babyhood and early childhood is the period of life in which we are most vulnerable to the world but also in which we are the most protected. The moon exerts its influences over babyhood, which seems wrapped in gentleness, a protective field of joy, spontaneity and the fantasy of the imaginary worlds. This is a world of fluidity where one thing can easily merge into another, one feeling into another, one experience into another and the sensory world provides a continous flow of smells, images and sensations so brilliantly captured by James Joyce in his novel *Portrait of a Young Man* as he recollects his early childhood:

> Once upon a time, and a very good time it was, there was a moocow coming down along the road, and this moocow that was coming down along the road met a nicens little boy named baby tuckoo. . . . His father told him that story: his father looked at him through a glass: he had a hairy face. He was a baby tuckoo. The moocow came down the road...

The emotional fluidity of this phase means that infants experience emotions fleetingly. The little child moves quickly from tears to pleasure and from sadness to joy and is easily distracted from one emotion to another, particularly if fantasy stories are used to inspire the child with new pictures of the new emotional place. Young children have great receptivity to the world around them, learning to speak and walk through imitation of those around them. The core building block is an unquestionable trust in the mother, the parents and the child's world to meet their needs. This is especially so in the first two years when the baby is extremely vulnerable and dependent for basic survival on the adults around them. During babyhood, the child should be protected from conflict, discord, negative words, actions and imagery as much as possible. The child is unable to assimilate traumatic experiences and they remain undigested in the child's emotional life, ultimately causing serious disturbances in adolescence and adulthood.

This golden period of early childhood and babyhood is a wonderful time for the young child to take in a variety of sensory impressions and through imitation learn to walk, talk and stand. The healthiest sensory impressions are those associated with nature and which reflect the natural rhythms. Rhythmical patterns are core to a happy, healthy babyhood and early childhood, so that the child develops patterns of eating, sleeping and playing in accord with the seasons and nature around them. The electronic world with its fast flashing lights, loud noises and passive engagement is the antithesis of what the child needs during this phase of development. Such media over-stimulate the child resulting in nervous exhaustion, inner depletion, irritability due to the loss of the natural bodily breathing rhythms which are so important for physical and emotional health in this age group. In contrast, a walk in the park, a swing in the park, a paddle in the ocean or a play outdoors will quickly restore the natural breathing rhythms of the irritable toddler or young child. The moon is the mother of many of our earthly rhythms and the young child shares this strong need for a patterned lifestyle to create contentment. Among traditional Aboriginal communities once noted for their rhythmical lifestyles, it has been shown that children from families owning televisions, who are more affluent, actually have poorer physical health and delayed physical growth compared to indigenous families with no television where children amuse themselves in the natural world (Peterson, 2010).

Physical development

The child grows faster at this period than at any other phase of the life span, usually doubling its weight by four months and reaching half their adult height by two years (Peterson, 2010, p.111). Between 2-4 years, the child grows in breadth and between 5-7 years in height. In addition, the proportion of the lower limbs to the head and trunk changes radically as illustrated on next page by Starts (Lievegoed, 2005, p.29).

During this period of development, the time spent sleeping declines rapidly as the young child spends time awake and interacting with the environment and its carers. Maturation, practice and hereditary ability combine

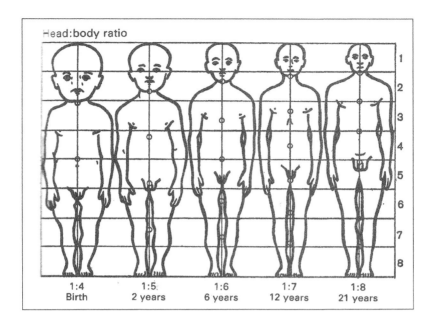

Head:body ratio

1:4	1:5	1:6	1:7	1:8
Birth	2 years	6 years	12 years	21 years

to influence at precisely what age a young child acquires certain motor skills. Peterson (2010, p.114) summarises these below:

The sequence of motor skill development during infancy

Motor skill	Average infant develops skill at	90% of infants have it by
Lifts head when prone	3 months	4 months
Sits with support	4 months	5 months
Rolls over from stomach to back	4 months	6 months
Sits without support	6 months	7.8 months
Walks holding on	9 months	13 months
Walks alone well	12.5 months	14.3 months
Walks backwards	18 months	21.5 months
Kicks ball	20 months	24 months

Source: Bayley (1993); Frankenberg & Dodds (1967); Shirley (1933).

By the age of seven months, babies develop the capacity to see the details of the human face. It is common for babies at eight months to cry when left with persons with whom they were previously happy and to want to remain with the mother, unless she is not the primary care giver.

Psychological: Cognitive development

The primary need of the young child is to develop their imaginative life. They do not have logic and cannot understand in logical causal terms what causes something. I remember my nephew at five years old going to the doctor with a sore eye and the doctor asked him what he thought caused it. My nephew replied:

> I was walking along the beach and a little thing, like a beetle with many legs got into my big toe. Then it travelled up inside my legs through my tummy and into my neck. It could not see there because it had small eyes, so it decided to move up and live in my eye. Then my eye started to hurt...

In addition, a number of understandings that adults take for granted are not part of the fantasy world in which the young child lives. They do not usually acquire a sense that their gender is fixed until 5-6 years, or that death is permanent until 4-5 years old (Peterson, 2010, p.122-3). The toddler and young child are not responsible for their deeds. They develop their morality at an unconscious level by absorbing the behaviours and deeds of the adults around them, so parental and carer modelling and behaviour is the single most important influence. Imitation is their major learning tool.

Young children do not tell falsehoods in this phase because the distinction between the physical and fantasy worlds is blurred and they lack logic. Parents bring their 4-5 year olds to counselling very upset that the child is "lying" to them, unaware the child does not have the same mental structures as an adult. I remember a distraught mother of four-year-old twin girls bringing them to counselling because they had taken red lipstick, drawn on the bedroom wall and scribbled on their new jackets. They insisted it was blood not lipstick. They were insistent the wall was hurt and their jackets were bleeding too. The mother was convinced they were outright liars and wanted me to sort them out and teach them to speak the truth, an impossible and inappropriate task at this developmental age.

Psychological: Emotional/social development

The baby's emotional life is primarily determined by their physical organism. They cry because they have a tummy ache or are wet, cold or hungry. The sensory life revolves around their bodily feelings. However, by toddlerhood, the outside world of the senses also profoundly influences their feelings. Here the child is at first unconscious of their perceptions and interprets the world entirely from the reactions and gestures of those in his or her environment. A toddler seeing a cat for the first time will assess how the adults react to the cat before deciding whether to laugh or cry, show fear or ignore the cat. The environment of fear and joy, trust and doubt created by the parents in the first years of life has profound effects on the emotional development of the child at the subconscious level, so that in adulthood they may act out of these subconscious places. Lievegoed (2009, p.57) describes it lucidly:

> Whether a person goes through life with an unwavering trust in the goodness of the world as the foundation of their spiritual life, despite any number of trials and tribulations, or whether they go through life filled with suspicion and lacking in joy, even though everything has gone their way, these things can be greatly influenced by the environment created by parents during the first years of life. People influence children during the first years of life by what they are, by expressing the trust they have acquired and morality in their actions.

The child's own feelings emerge when they withdraw for the first time from exclusively experiencing the world according to their bodily sensations and create their own structured emotional world where they are the creator of the meaning of their experience (Lievegoed, 2005, p.72). As long as the young child's play is performed rhythmically in relation to the child's natural breathing, the child does not tire. It is a-rhythmical activities and the intellectual and cognitive demands that tire young children. Early intellectual activities are unhealthy for the young child's development and lead to loss of imaginative, creative abilities as well as deplete the growing child's body unnecessarily. At approximately five to six years of age, the child develops their own will in the sense of their capacity to change consciously the physical environment around them. They develop respect for the person who can best shape the physical world in ways that matter to the child, whether as a parent mending a toy or a family friend who can make a boat. With respect comes the first strong recognition of authority, that there are those who can perform with greater success and exert their will more effectively in the world. Respect develops in the child by viewing the behavioural competence of adults who demonstrate to the young child their abilities to create and sustain physical things in the world through good deeds (Lievegoed, 2005). Respect needs to be earned by adults. It is incongruent to expect a child to "choose to respect" an adult who has not earned the child's respect through their moral deeds in the world.

The individual child's response to the environment around them is determined by cultural norms. For example, Aboriginal babies cry less, are more able to soothe themselves and less startled by noises. They are also more alert at birth and their motor development is earlier than their white counterparts (Peterson, 2010). Hereditary factors are very important and identical twins display very similar temperament.

Attachment or trust in the primary care giver is the primary pattern in the first two years that has profound consequences for all future relationships in the person's life. Secure attachment is ideal and here the baby weeps when the mother leaves and is delighted when she returns. The mother is sensitive and responsive to the baby's needs. This creates a secure foundation for later childhood and adulthood. Such a person is more willing to take risks, has greater resilience when something fails, has higher self-esteem and is confident in creating, maintaining and being present to social and intimate relationships.

The baby, who experiences insecure attachment, is indifferent to the presence or absence of the mother and tends in life to give up more readily when challenged, lacks confidence in social relationships and is likely to retreat when intimate relationships are difficult. They lack trust and confidence in the human world.

Finally, the anxious, avoidant, attached child receives erratic parenting, sometimes being loved and having its needs met and at other times, always unpredictable, being rejected, ignored or abused. These children grow up with anxiety about the world of relationships and are likely to pursue others even when relationships are obviously destructive, such as in domestic violence relationships. These babies cling to their mothers and cry when they leave but do not show joy on their return. This is also a classic characteristic of conflicted adult relationships driven by anxiety and fear of abandonment (Petersen, 2010). Healthy social-emotional development is dependent on the early attachment experiences and it cannot be overemphasized because many adults presenting in therapy do so because of fracturing in the early bonding relationships with their primary carer.

Spiritual development

The experience of the self, the place from which the child's own spirit is to emanate does not first appear strongly until the child is at its first moon node (2.3 years of age) within the first seven-year life span. This is hailed by the use of the word "I". Previously, the young child only uses their name or refers to themselves in the third person, such as "Johnny wants to swing higher"... which is now replaced by "I want to swing higher". It is the true beginning of self-awareness (O'Neil &O'Neil, 1998, p.298). It is also usually the beginning of conscious memory. Few children can recall events prior to the first experience of using the word "I" to refer to themselves. At this point, one could say the unique "I" or spirit of the child is making a big step into the child's body and this should be celebrated. However, for the weary parent having a two-year old direct what they will eat, wear and do can be inconvenient to say the least. Most exhausted parents of two-year olds occasionally wonder why they ever taught them to say "no" as it is the favourite word of the incarnating "I" of the two-year old. However, if the "no" is seen as a "yes" to the beginnings of a space for the development of their own unique spirit, the parent can creatively find ways to embrace it, while still accomplishing the day-to-day activities that need to be fulfilled. The "terrible twos" become the "terrific twos", at least for some of the time.

The next 2.3-year cycle culminates close to the fifth birthday of the child when it begins to ask "why" about everything, as the child's consciousness starts to embrace the wider world beyond its self and its family. I remember at this time explaining very authoritatively to everyone I met the difference between a television aerial and a TV aerial based on having questioned two adults about the name for this wire standing on top of houses in my street. It just happened that one type of wire was square the other rectangular, and I had made this differentiation based upon their answers to my "why" question and my observation of the different shapes of aerials, which was actually irrelevant to the two adults. Like many 5-6 year olds, I spoke very authoritatively on something which was actually factually wrong believing there to be some real distinction between a TV aerial and a television aerial.

Developmental decisions

When is a child ready for school?

The child is ready for school when the physical body has slimmed down to represent the figure on page 23, at six years and no longer has the toddler figure. The limbs have a growth spurt and represent the will or the young child's capacity to shape the world around them. In addition, the child should have started to lose their milk teeth. The emergence of the adult teeth represents the anchoring of the thinking forces in the child's body. Children are not ready to learn to read until they lose the front milk teeth and start developing the adult teeth.

Why do young children become anxious?

Children under the age of seven are like one large sensory organ taking in all the impressions around them. The young child flourishes when the sensory world around them is peaceful, quiet, rhythmical and harmonious with their rhythmical breathing and the images are beautiful, gentle and protective. Young children exposed to startling noises, violence, flickering lights, fast moving electronic media– particularly with disturbing or aggressive images– are flooded by processes that their immature nervous systems and cognitive faculties cannot process. This then can lead to fear and anxiety in the young child (Staley, 1997). The flooding by electronic imagery is particularly indigestible to the child. The remedy lies in recreating a safe sensory environment for the young child and using therapies that are gentle, such as spontaneous sand play, so that the child can work through its fears and build a new foundation based on protection and rhythm.

Why do young children lie so much and deny that they have done things?

Children this age do not have an understanding of cause and effect and they live in a world of fantasy where everything is possible, and this world is more real than the physical world. They also live out a sense of animism whereby inanimate objects are as real or more real than living persons. The teddy bear is a case in point. A child will be inconsolable if their teddy bear is left behind, regardless of how kind mum and dad are at that moment. A pushbike may be seen as a person and invisible friends are common. Even objects like the sun and the moon may easily be given faces and names. Their actions are largely driven by immediate bodily impulses with no reflection or insight on consequences.

What is the easiest way to discipline a toddler and a young child in this age group?

Firstly, a child learns good behaviour through imitation and modelling the desired behaviour through your own actions and speech. Secondly, they learn when you use purposeful distractions whereby you distract their attention from the undesirable situation to a new desirable situation. Thirdly, when you enter the world of fantasy in which they live and use active fantasy images to achieve the outcome that a parent sometimes needs to achieve is another way to impart good behaviour.

Example One: Johnny is two years old and is playing with trains and you need to give him lunch in order to attend afternoon playgroup by 1pm. Instead of: "Johnny come and eat your lunch now" (he will say NO most likely) relate to his fantasy world..."Toot toot...Tommy the tank engine is coming to collect his carriages to refuel" and become Tommy the tank engine coming to collect him for lunch... Make the lunch table the refuelling stop so Tommy the tank engine gets a sandwich too.

Example Two: Mary is four years old and screaming at breakfast because there are no cornflakes left, only Wheatbix, and she is inconsolable. Telling Mary you will buy her some cornflakes when you next go shopping is too logical and will not help her. Rather, solve the problem by entering her fantasy world of imaginative thought. Pick up something that can act as a magic wand, go to Mary, and say...let's turn the Wheatbix into cornflakes and start waving the wand over the Wheatbix saying magic words like abracadabra etc. etc...Get her to join in...magically turning the Wheatbix into cornflakes. There is a very high chance she will now happily eat the Wheatbix that have become magical cornflakes.

When should a child speak in sentences?

Talking varies a great deal among different children and it is a process of development that begins with babble in the early months. The baby gradually moves to one word communication with a very limited vocabulary around 12 months. By two years, most children can say simple sentences although the sentences are mostly incomplete. By four years old young children can make themselves understood with sentences quite clearly, although they still make errors and their vocabulary is limited. It is more common for the first child to speak earlier because of the need to communicate directly with adults and for the younger children to be slower because they can baby speak with siblings and still be understood. It is also more common for children of middle-class families to speak more than children from lower socio-economic classes where language is less central to the family communication system.

Conclusion

The period from birth to seven years is a profoundly important period. During this phase, the physical developmental forces work profoundly to develop the core human capacities of standing on two legs, walking on two legs, talking and thinking. Under the influence of the moon, the watery, malleable, soft, cuddly baby is developmentally being shaped by the formative life forces at the most rapid rate of all of the life span. During the first two years, the head predominates, then during the following three years the trunk predominates and finally between 5-7 years the limbs predominate arriving at the limb dominance that is characteristic of adult humans. The development of language links the young child socially, emotionally and spiritually with the human community, and in particular the culture that shapes the soul of his first language. Play develops from solitary, to alongside others around two years of age and to cooperative play from around four years of age, as the young child becomes part of the social world. In terms of the child's human spirit, there is the profound announcement at 2.3 years that "I am here". It is this "I" that is the carrier of the unique being of the child within its growing human body. It flowers from a seed in the baby to an oak tree by 63 years, given the conditions to nurture this development.

SUMMARY

- I am growing so rapidly especially in the first year of life that excellent nutrition is critical for building the foundations of my physical body.

- I need to be securely attached to my caregiver so I can trust the world into which I have been born and build healthy relationships in my life based upon my first experience of trust.

- I am vulnerable to loud noises, flashing lights and discordant sounds and am happier when my environment is peaceful and calm with subtle and beautiful sensory experiences.

- I need to have a rhythmical life to grow and feel well nourished. I am happier if I eat and sleep following regular routines.

- I flourish if I can safely explore the natural environment rather than being exposed to the electronic world so early in my life.

- I live in a beautiful world of fantasy and I do not distinguish between the physical world and my fantasy world. They all blur together.

- My teddies and my dolls, my bike and my spade are also like people with feelings and faces and are precious to me.

- I do not understand logic, cause and effect but I can make magic and understand magic and fantasy so remember to explain things to me with magic. Remember, I am not yet rational.

- I love the beauty and magic of my fantasy world. I cannot digest ugliness or horror in pictures or in my life. They remain deeply hidden in me and arise in my adolescent and/or adult life to cause me turmoil. As a child, I often have to act them out to get them out of myself.

- I learn from the moral tone of your speaking and acting in the world. It goes deeply into my unconscious and shapes my future deeds in the world.

- If I am feeling fearful in any way I quickly excarnate or leave my body so that my spirit is not damaged by the traumas happening around me. However, while this helps me survive a difficult childhood, it is a bad habit to take into adulthood because it stops me being present to solve problems in difficult times.

- I need to know that my parents are in charge and that they will make decisions for me out of love even if I do not always like them.

- I need to be warm; I do not always feel when my little body is cold.

REFERENCES

Bryant, W (1993) *The Veiled Pulse of Time: Life cycles and Destiny,* NY, Lindisfarne.

Lievegoed, B (2003) *Phases: The Spiritual Rhythms in Adult Life,* London, Sophia Books.

Lievegoed, B (2005) *Phases of Childhood: Growing in Body, Soul and Spirit,* Edinburgh, Floris.

O'Neil, G & O'Neil, G (1998) *The Human Life,* NY, Mercury Press.

Peterson, C (2010) *Looking Forward through the Lifespan: Developmental Psychology,* Sydney, Pearson.

Staley, B (1997) *Tapestries:Weaving Life's Journey,* Stroud, Hawthorn press.

Children have never been very good at listening to their elders
but they have never failed to imitate them.

—James Baldwin

CHAPTER 3

Exploring the known world: 7-14 years

Introduction

This is the most vibrant and healthy phase of the human life cycle, when children have boundless energy to participate in the world and to explore their potential with enthusiasm and vigour. Mercury with its dynamic energy profoundly influences this period providing much of the energy to explore and understand the physical world around them. It also ensures they recover quickly from stress (O'Neil & O'Neil, 1998). In the early part of this phase from 7-9 years, the young child is still living largely out of their creativity and "covered by the merciful veil of his own imagination" (Lievegoed, 2005, p.83). They do not yet have abstract ideas nor do they think abstractly, but the child's will is awakening to the world and to shaping the world. Erikson describes this phase as "industry versus inferiority". The child needs to achieve in the world around them and this is critical for the child's sense of developing self. During this childhood period, profound thinking changes occur, including the development of rudimentary logic and the capacity for one-to-one correspondence when counting or describing things. The concrete realities of the material world start to dominate the child's thinking.

There are also the core moon-node transitions at the ninth and one third year, in which the child first experiences itself as a totally separate person in the world. The glow of their early childhood now fades as they become firmly grounded in day-to-day realities and their natural joy and spontaneity starts to be tinged with routine, ordinariness and at times boredom. This again is a core landmark of the "I" becoming more firmly anchored in the child's body. The child's spirit, which in the 0-7 phase could readily leave the child's body and hover well above the child's consciousness, is now less able to excarnate or leave the child's body when faced with conflict or traumatic situations. There is now a tendency for the child's "I" or spirit to disappear and hide within the child's body. Typical places for disappearing are behind the heart, behind the ear, at the top of the head or the tip of the feet. This disappearance is a primitive strategy used by the growing child to protect its spirit from damage arising from trauma. These processes are detailed in Sherwood (2007).

Another core incarnating point for the child's "I" is eleven and two-thirds years old when the child starts to enter the pubescent phase of development. Gender differences become obvious with girls' bodies gradually becoming rounder and softer than boys' bodies. In boys, the larynx starts to elongate and their voice to deepen in stark contrast to the high pitched giggling of girls in this age group (Staley, 1993). Many of the problems of adolescence have roots in unresolved issues during this 7-14 year phase of development.

Physical development

The growth energy in this period is first located in the respiratory organs then moves down the body to focus on the reproductive system. Thus, in this phase, we see the enlargement of the heart and the lungs, the four-to-one ratio of pulse and breath, and the beginnings of sexual maturity (Bryant, 1993). As with all development, there is always a normal distribution curve so, for example, some girls may have their first period "the menarche" as early as nine or ten years old while other girls may not have their first period until 16 years of age. The average is 13 years of age.

Between seven and 12 the child's head reaches the proportion of one-to-seven and is very close to the final adult proportions of one-to-eight (Lievegoed, 2009, p.84). The brain grows from 90 per cent its size at six years to its full size during this phase. Obesity and diabetes are the dominant serious illnesses in this age group, both of them largely lifestyle engendered through lack of exercise and poor diet. Obesity can result in adult health problems as well as disadvantage the child socially and psychologically, depending on the particular culture and its values (Peterson, 2010). Electronically based activities account for a significant cause of obesity in Australia with children spending an average of 28 hours on electronic media per fortnight, and only six hours on sporting activities during school time. (Peterson, 2010,p.269). Physical abilities like throwing a ball, running, hopping and skipping accelerate in speed and skill during this phase of development and they make an important contribution to the child's self-esteem and social acceptance.

From 13-14 years of age, the adolescent growth spurt that started between 11 and 12 years is in rapid progress. Girls mature two years earlier than boys, and at 12 and 13 years of age most girls are bigger than boys and stronger. I recall a 12-year-old boy complaining to me about the school discipline procedures: "It is not fair that we get into trouble if we hit the girls who tease us, because they are bigger and stronger than we are..." However, so much of a girl's energy goes into growth and development at this early phase that they often respond by withdrawing from the world, forming their own groups of peers and they become reduced to giggling and gossiping about others. Their sense of strength in the world and self-esteem plummets. Often these changes result in a latent hostility in girls, which is projected onto parents and teachers and unfortunate siblings.

Boys on the other hand, start their growth spurt later and are more likely to act out in the world their frustrations and confusions. Unlike girls, they are brimming with energy to expend in the world and this energy needs to be directed towards constructive activities, particular in relation to sport, gym, music and drama (Lievegoed, 2010). Wilderness activities and physical challenges led by men are to be particularly recommended. Rock and Water is such a program that is well suited for this age group (*www.rockandwaterprogram.com/*). Sherwood (2013) documents the range of non-verbal activities such as wilderness therapy, music therapy, drama therapy, art therapy that work well with adolescents facing a range of mental health issues.

Psychological: Cognitive development

The emphasis during this period from 7-14 years, is on developing literacy and numeracy skills as well as developing an understanding of the rules and norms of the school environment in which they now spend the majority of their waking hours. One of the most profound cognitive changes the child makes is movement from pre-operational to concrete operational thinking, which means the ability to conserve length, area, weight and numbers. This profound change in cognitive abilities was identified by Piaget as occurring at approximately seven years of age (Peterson, 2010). Some concrete examples of this change is that the child is now able to understand that a banana cut into six pieces constitutes the same amount as a whole banana. The child now understands that regardless of the size or the shape of the glass, if the same amount of water is poured from a jug into the glass, it is the same quantity of water. Physical appearances are now overridden with logic. A child begins to understand one-to-one correspondence, which is essential to counting. However, the exact time at which this change occurs depends on the child's culture and the nature of the teaching curriculum. For example, a Pueblo Indian child exposed to clay from early childhood and watching parents making utensils, can tell you as early as four years of age that the amount of clay is the same in two different shapes. If the school system emphasises cognitive performance then children are more likely to make the transition earlier than if the school system promotes imaginative creative play and art as the priority. Unpublished research on comparing a sample of children aged seven, eight and nine for conservation tasks in a government school and an anthroposophical school, showed that on all conservation tasks the children made the transition at a later age in the anthroposophical school which emphasizes creativity and imagination (Sherwood, 1990).

During primary school years, there is a rapid increase in children's problem solving abilities in relation to concrete tasks placed before them. They develop a new raft of cognitive skills including thinking strategically, giving selective attention to relevant details and memory storage and retrieval skills that are consciously directed toward a particular event or task. Many of these skills are profoundly influenced by the home environment and relationship between children and parents. For example, a girl's ability in this age group to solve real-life problems has been found to be directly related to a father's presence in the girl's life. Fry and Gover showed that interaction with the father increases a girl's ability to generate ideas, her persistence in problem solving, her attention and her achievements in problem solving (Peterson, 2010).

A child's reading ability and comprehension becomes a critical tool in the school environment but the emphasis on reading by 6-7 years is, according to the anthroposophical model of education, better replaced by introducing reading at the time of the loss of milk teeth and the emergence of the secondary teeth. This better allows for identifying when the child is ready to read, given the wide variety of developmental patterns in this middle childhood phase.

Significant differences have been found in children's performances independent of actual intelligence and academic ability in this age phase. Dweck labelled these mastery orientation versus self-defeating personality types. Self-defeating children suffer from learned helplessness, take a passive self-defeating attitude to tasks even before they commence, give up easily, misunderstand feedback and demonstrate self-defeating reasoning that dismisses their abilities or achievements. Mastery orientated children, in contrast, confront obstacles with confidence, tend not to contemplate causes for difficulties and focus their attention on problem solving (Peterson, 2010). The reasons for this self-defeating attitude may include family system patterns, early child attachment patterns, teacher-child relationships, sibling issues or temperament.

The temperaments

In the anthroposophical model of education and development, there are four types of temperaments. These are melancholic, choleric, sanguine and phlegmatic. The melancholic child tends to the self-defeating pattern believing that it is overwhelmingly difficult even before beginning a task and giving up easily or collapsing into tears at the thought of completing an assigned task. The best parent-teacher strategy with this child is positive encouragement, to work with the child to achieve task completion and to counter the child's self-deprecating talk with positive affirmation. The sanguine child is usually happy and delighted with the world, approaches tasks enthusiastically but is easily distracted with more interesting activities or ideas. This child is very optimistic in their approach to new experiences but needs parental and teacher help to stay focused on the task and needs to be rewarded for completing a task because focusing their will is an important developmental feature for such children. In contrast, the choleric child is will driven and very focused on the task and often demonstrates a high level of mastery orientation. They often are the first finished and the most confident. The downside of this temperament is their bossiness, the need to organise everyone else to follow their directions and issue commands to others to complete the task. Choleric children know exactly how to do the task, and advice from parents or teachers is regarded as an intrusion, interrupting their flow of completion. Choleric children need reminders from people they love and respect to feel into their hearts and to be sensitive to the feelings of other children who are different to themselves. Finally, the phlegmatic child is very slow moving and usually does not finish assigned tasks, not because of self-defeating attitudes, but simply because they need so much longer to complete tasks than other children because getting started and being motivated to engage in the physical world is always a struggle. If someone else will do it, they are usually content. It is important to give these children more time to complete tasks and not to step in and take over, however tempting this may be at times. The four temperaments with both their positive and negative qualities help one to understand how the tasks of this age group are approached differently by different children (Cocoris, 2009).

Psychological: Social and emotional development

Seven years of age is a landmark in the child's social and emotional development as the child becomes content for the first time in its life to leave its mother for longer periods as it seeks to spend time exploring the world of its peers (Lievegoed, 2009). During this age, the child creates strong relationships with its peers, and belonging to a group of friends is important for the child's sense of social development. The qualities that make for peer popularity in this age group are outgoing friendly temperaments, good social skills, sensitivity to other people's feelings, the ability to create and maintain harmonious social relationships within the peer group and the ability to share common interests with other members of the peer group (Peterson, 2010). Children rejected or excluded by peers generally demonstrate low levels of social skills, low empathy and poor interpersonal sensitivity, and are often aggressive or hostile towards other children. Commonly, they manifest at school the dysfunctional skills of one or more members of their family system.

Early in this period children accept gender permanence, recognising the clear physical distinction between girls and boys, which is reinforced by the schooling system. However, they will still quite happily play with each other in the 7-8 year period but between 9-10 years of age, the gender lines are drawn by children and strongly reinforced from 11-14 years as children's bodies change in radical ways to reflect gender difference. When asked if they were willing to play with boys at school the following replies were received from different age groups of girls:

Eight years: "Yes, they are ok to play with but they are not my favourite."
Ten years old. "No, they are boys and they smell."
Thirteen years old: "Yes, I like talking to and spending time with some boys."

Unfortunately, electronic media continue to project stereotypical images of males and females, and the best counter to this influence is parental modelling. Children tend to identify with the same sex parent and that identification has a profound effect on the child's understanding of gender and gender roles.

Electronic media and an excess focus on cognitive activities during this phase of development, stultify the development of the child's creative artistic spirit. This carries the feeling life of the child and should be the core focus in primary school. It is most important that primary school children develop their creativity through arts, writing, handicrafts, gardening and their interaction with nature. During this period, the creative forces are the primary developmental need for the child. Overemphasis on cognitive performance stultifies the creative forces, produces unhappy, unfulfilled children who find school boring or stressful and who tend to withdraw from the learning process at any given opportunity. If the creative, problem solving, innovative energy in this age group is ignored or repressed, not only does it produce emotionally, unhappy children – some of whom misbehave – but it also dampens these problem-solving forces for life and part of the great potential of this child is buried. It is almost impossible to resurrect it as an adult (Lievegoed, 2009). An overemphasis on cognitive performance at the expense of recognising and developing the natural feeling life of the child, in later years distorts their adult knowledge and familiarity with their feeling life. Bryant (1993, p.63) describes the problem:

> The intrusion, which many call education, merely marches legions of sterile facts across the fertile garden of imagination and feeling. No wonder the stunted feeling of so many adults require multitudes of psychiatrists to solve problems that should never have arisen. An education, which takes into account the need for emotional exercise, helps to promote a healthy emotional rapport between intellect and emotions, and between self and social world.

Spiritual development

Building the child's sense of self and strengthening their unique spirit is the most critical task because it lays the foundation for the child's self-esteem, not only in these middle years but for ongoing developmental phases. This means making a concerted effort to find what the child loves doing and to support the child to do this in their life whether it be music, dance, drama, sport, art, caring for pets, gardening or playing chess. Any of a host of ways in which the unique human spirit in a child connects the child to the physical world and builds their self-esteem is to be valued.

Failure to do this leads to what Erikson termed "inferiority" (Peterson, 2010, p.240), a core paving stone for low self-esteem. Ironically, the research by Robins et al (2002, p.428) which comprised interviews of 326,641 individuals about their self-esteem, showed that girls and boys report the same high levels of self-esteem between nine and 12 years old but on average girls' levels of self-esteem start plummeting around 13 years of age, dropping twice as much as boys' self-esteem. It remains substantially lower than male self-esteem throughout the lifespan. Only at the 80-year age bracket do females and males self-esteem coincide again, and for the first time at 85 years of age, females exceed males in self-esteem. The reasons for this have been widely debated but one perspective is that cultural values favour patriarchal dominant male values such as science, logic, materialism, objects, and under-value dominant feminine attributes and abilities such as caring, creativity, cooperation and the arts.

This 7-14 bracket is also the period in which the child is internalising moral guidelines for behaviour. In this age group, there is significant development of a conscience, of learning the rules and doing the right thing, which promotes ethical behaviour. Children in this age phase are capable of resisting temptation, feeling guilt, knowing the rules, confessing to wrongdoing and making restitution for their wrong deeds(Hoffman cited in Peterson, 2010). Many children from 5-10 years old usually do what is right because they fear punishment or rejection if they do not. It is the good boy/good girl syndrome of stage three moral development when children do things because it is the rules and to be good one must follow the rules.

The critical moon node of nine and two-thirds influences the tenth year of development profoundly and the child's moral reasoning. The child starts to ask critical questions, becomes gradually aware of their own flaws and the flaws of people around them, including parents and teachers. Their protective childhood bubble of creative imagination, which has protected them, has well and truly burst and the fears and ugliness of the world begin to enter their world. The child experiences its self as cut-off from others, of standing alone in the world for the first time in his/her life. At this point, the child may become fearful of a range of things from insects, to war, to losing their family to death and destruction. It is important that images and stories that now include the war between good and evil end happily with good triumphing. Morally, the child cannot digest a world in which evil prevails. That is the challenge of adolescence. This crisis is best handled by directing the child's attention to nature, the beauty and patterns in the natural kingdom, and introducing the child to archetypes of goodness, truth, beauty, warriors who fight for the light, or represent aspects of it. This provides the greatest emotional stability for the child's spirit (Lievegoed 2005).

During this period, the unique spirit of the child, continues to dissociate or leave the child's body if confronted by fearful threats, cold rejection, horror or unassimilable evil. The child manifests this in a variety of ways including glazed looks on their face, shaking, rapid breathing and stomach aches, and in some extreme cases in self-mutilating behaviours. There is a need to restore the heart's rhythm through deep breathing, stamping feet, drumming or some activity that brings the child's spirit back to their body. Activities to achieve this are presented in *Emotional Literacy*, a handbook of exercises for rebalancing the child's body, heart and mind (Sherwood, 2008).

While the school age child sets themselves small tasks and goals to achieve in the world, from 12 to 14 years the child's will to take his place in the world dominates and the tasks now become the focus of his life. It is important to direct children's thinking at this age towards the totality of the world, so they can find their connection to the world. Ideally, this is the time when they come to think about how they will bring their unique gift of their spirit to the world. Children who have low self-esteem do not have a sense of their unique spirit or gift. They are left in the morass of disconnection from the world and can easily fall prey to either self-harm, suicidal ideation or to aggressive destructive behaviours against the world, such as vandalism. It is the role of culture and the parent to help the child create this self-esteem bridge to cross into the world at adolescence.

Developmental decisions

How does one manage the teacher's opinions that my child accepts but I disagree with, particularly in relation to right behaviour?

It may be most helpful to have a conversation with the teacher about why they require certain behaviours in the classroom so you can better understand why this is necessary. However, if you and the teacher are unable to find a middle pathway of agreement, then the child needs to have it clearly explained to them that there are different rules in these two different places, home and school. Children at this stage of development need only a few very clear rules with very clear consequences.

What is the best parenting style for this age group?

Research shows the best parenting style is one in which parents set firm and sensible rules and monitor these via open parent-child communication, and when the parents' discipline is warm and loving. The old adage "firm and loving" suits this age group well. In addition, it is important with this age group to teach the child clear boundaries regarding the rights of others and respect for them, not only through rules but by modelling the behaviours you wish your children to demonstrate in their lives. This style of parenting leads to better school grades across the transition to high school rather than other types of parenting (Peterson, 2010, p.233). The children from such parents also show higher levels of social competency than children with uninvolved or hostile parents.

What is the best management strategy to stop or reduce the high level of fights between siblings in this age group?

Treating both children with the same levels of affection and applying the same levels of disciplinary control is the greatest contributor to reducing fights between siblings. Siblings at this age see parental preference for one child as a sign they are unworthy of their love and express this as resentment and hostility towards the favoured sibling. Simultaneously, it is important to recognise and encourage individual differences in abilities among children at this age and to reward children based on their individual abilities, not on some abstract goal. Fairness is a very important value for children in this age group. Fairness means clear rules that are applied in the same manner to all children of the same age. Fairness also means punishments are in proportion to the offence and reflect accurately the level of misdemeanour. Fairness also means the child can understand and predict how rules will be applied to their behaviour and there is no manipulation of the rules or hidden agendas.

How do I deal with my child's daydreaming?

Children daydream to hold onto the protective fantasy world of early childhood or to escape from boredom or environments in which they feel stressed or fearful. Unfortunately, school systems generally have a strong cognitive and performance ethic, which is often forced upon children between six and nine years. Often children in these age groups are not yet ready to achieve some school tasks. It is important that in middle childhood, children have plenty of engagement in activities in the natural environment from swinging, to building houses, to climbing trees. In the natural environment the child has the space to transit naturally into the demands of cognitive and physical task completion. Children are still emerging from the otherworldly experience of early childhood and it is important to remember it takes time to transit from egg to pupae to butterfly. Some children, particularly those with widely spaced eyes and broad foreheads, will take much longer to come to terms with the physical realities and demands of school, than those children with close set eyes and close set features who are very ready to tackle the physical world and negotiate the school system.

The two different types of children are well represented in the introductory picture to this chapter. They both happen to be looking at the first camera they have seen that takes pictures that you can see instantly on a miniscreen. The little blonde haired girl has come across from her seat in the car to her brother's side, to ask questions about it although she is only six years old. The boy who is nine years old is tentatively asking questions but is still overshadowed by his very present and incarnated sister. He could still spend hours daydreaming or playing quiet games in his own imaginary world, while she was organising the physical world and the people around her. She is proficient at managing other people and directing their activities at every opportunity. Daydreaming types of children between seven and 10 years usually need less pressure to perform academically and more time to grow up gently and gradually in the world of nature and their own imaginations. Pressuring these children to perform creates emotional and physical stresses on their developing physical body and is likely to result in health issues, low self-esteem and a sense of being overwhelmed.

Conclusion

This critical phase of middle childhood commencing at seven years of age and ending with pubescence between 12-14 years, marks a remarkable change in the child's relationship with themselves, other children and the world. Not only do most children grow to almost their full adult height, but also during this period they experience the emergence of secondary sexual characteristics which creates in them a very different orientation to their bodies and their peers. They break out of the cocoon of the protective imaginative world of childhood in which they are immersed to the realities of the physical world around them. They have tasks to be accomplished in that world and problems to be resolved.

During this phase their high levels of creativity and imagination should be nurtured strongly through the arts, contact with the environment and through creative activities which involve active engagement in the physical world. Keeping these qualities vibrant is fundamental to the happiness of their future development as they nurture the feeling life and their creativity. Premature emphasis on cognitive achievements dulls the feeling life and creativity, and these qualities may never be fully recovered in adult life leading to unsatisfactory intimate relationships and family life. Children at this developmental phase become "god's policemen", and in the early stage insist that the rules are followed by everyone, including their parents. Following the 9-10 year old crisis in which they come to experience themselves as a truly separate being in the world for the first time, the awareness of good and evil comes strongly into their consciousness. The feeling life transforms and the language of imagery now starts to be dominated by music. Lievegoed (2005, p.171) describes his process:

> After the age of 10, a great change occurs in feelings... Previously he lived mainly in images, now he enters a period of musicality and drama. The light and dark, which had appeared from the outside as good and evil, now starts to take part in his inner life.

It is critical at this phase they are presented with stories, both fact and fiction in which good triumphs over evil so they can feel secure in the world and so that their vulnerability is protected sufficiently for them to develop confidence in their safety in the world. It is also essential the child is supported to develop a connection to the wide world in terms of something the child loves – whether music, art, drama, sport or botany – that gives the child feelings of success, goodness and achievement which form the basis of their self-esteem. It is a sense of self-esteem, a strong feeling that I can bring my gift to the world whatever it is, that provides the critical bridge into adolescent when the core questions of "why I am here" and "who am I" will be asked.

SUMMARY

- I am growing quickly in my body so I need plenty of good rest and healthy, low sugar, low fat foods, lots of fresh fruit and vegetables, particularly greens which give me a healthy foundation for my adult weight and health. I need "nude food" not processed food for maximum health.

- I have to leave my world of childhood fantasy and imagination to creatively problem solve in the world but remember it takes some time and I will often not complete tasks, even simple ones to adult standards.

- I like having friends and spending time in groups, playing team games and learning to work with others but these social skills of cooperation, empathy and sensitivity take time to master and I learn them from home.

- I need to explore the physical and natural world with my parents to learn how to problem solve and complete tasks in the physical world.

- I like clear rules with clear consequences both at school and at home.

- I need to be exposed to images of darkness only in so far as they can be outweighed by images of goodness and the good always needs to win over the evil otherwise I can develop mental health problems like anxiety, now or in later developmental phases.

- I need to discover what I love doing in the world, what is the unique gift of my spirit so I can build strong self-esteem and focus in my life.

- I need to experience success at some tasks so I can build confidence in myself and contribute to my family and community.

- I can easily "disappear" into my body when I feel threatened or traumatised and my eyes are open and my mouth may move but I am not present to what is happening and I will not remember anything.

- I can also "disappear" if I am bored and I do not learn or remember because I am not present, not because I am unintelligent or stupid.

REFERENCES

Bryant, W (1993) *The Veiled Pulse of Time: Life Cycles &Destiny,* NY, Lindisfarne.

Cocoris, J (2009) *The Temperament Model of Behaviour: The Description of the Four Primary Temperaments. www.fourtemperaments.com/Description.htm accessed 21-01-13.*

Lievegoed, B (2005) *Phases of Childhood: Growing in Body, Soul and Spirit,* Edinburgh, Floris.

O'Neil, G& O'Neil, G (1998) *The Human Life,*NY, Mercury Press.

Peterson, C (2010) *Looking Forward through the Lifespan: Developmental Psychology,*Sydney, Pearson.

Robins, R, Trzesniewski, K, Tracy, J, Gosling, S, Potter, J (2002) Global self-esteem across the life span,*American Psychology and Aging*, Vol. 17(3) Sept, 2002. Pp.423-434 DOI: 10.1037/0882-7974.17.3.423

Sherwood, P (2013) *Emotional Literacy for Adolescent Mental Health: Expressive Therapies,* Melbourne,Acer.

Sherwood, P (2008) *Emotional Literacy: The Heart of Classroom Management*, Melbourne, Acer.

Sherwood, P (2007) *Holistic Counselling: A New Vision for Mental Health,* Bunbury, Sophia Publications.

Staley, B (1997) *Tapestries: Weaving Life's Journey,* Stroud, Hawthorn Press.

Adolescents are not monsters. They are just people trying to learn how to make it among the adults in the world, who are probably not so sure themselves.

Virginia Satir (1988)

CHAPTER 4

Adolescence 14-21 years
"Searching for yourself"

Introduction

Adolescence is the most turbulent phase of the whole life span as the movement from carefree childhood to responsible adult is both challenging and inspiring for the adolescent and significant adults in their life. Nor is progress to adulthood a straight line. The moments of demanding adult rights are followed by moments of sinking into childhood irresponsibility, which is confusing for both the adolescent, parents and the adults around them. The 14-21 year phase is characterised by three extremely important years in which a significant presence of the new emerging adult becomes visible to those around them; namely 16, 18 and 21 years of age. At these ages we see the unique individual start to emerge who may be a "stranger in our presence" or who may be somewhat familiar. Culturally, the emerging adult presence is recognised by the legal rights to have sex, leave home and marry at 16 years of age, to drive a car and vote by 18 years of age. By 21, the adult is characterised by physical maturity, and full reflective insightful consciousness, or "I", is assumed present. Of course, with prolonged education and economic dependency on families for most of this time, this level of maturity may not be achieved as quickly.

As the higher presence or "I" of the adult insightful consciousness manifests, the essential spirit of the person becomes present. They are now more competent to manage their lives but it also brings the potential for increased levels of anger. When a young child is feeling fearful or threatened they can readily disappear or dissociate as the presence of their spirit is only tenuously connected to their body. However, in adolescence the spirit of the person can no longer easily disappear and must confront the world in the body. Therefore, when the adolescent has a threatening or traumatic childhood, their feelings of childhood helplessness and trauma can be triggered easily by authoritarian adults– be they parents or teachers. Unlike the child who withdraws into themselves or dissociates, the adolescent is much more likely to fight back through anger. Our culture's primitive defence mechanism for fighting off threats is anger – either exploded or imploded. This exploded anger can be both intimidating and destructive to those around the adolescent. While boys tend to explode their anger in an outwardly violent manner, girls, in particular, often implode their anger and express it as bitchiness, gossip, ridicule and sarcasm. Moral development in adolescence demands authenticity, so it is challenging to bring an adolescent to counselling because they express anger when their mother and father also express anger. They will certainly notice the incongruity in moral standards and expectations and will not be impressed. It is essential an adult does not demand from an adolescent, behaviour they themselves are unable to manifest and model to them.

It is a phase when young people want not just role models, but heroes to inspire them with all that is good, beautiful and true. If these are not available, then they will chose heroes that inspire them even if it is with darkness, discord and ugliness. Where parents and schools fail to provide heroes, the media, particularly the music industry, step in because music becomes a core, developmental medium for adolescents to express their inner life. It is not surprising that music idols incorporate so much drama in their performances as these are the languages of the adolescent. Venus governs adolescence and, in particular, influences the arts and physical and erotic love which is at the heart of the adolescent transition into adulthood (O'Neil & O'Neil, 1998).

In addition, the 18-year rhythm of the moon profoundly influences the transition into young adulthood. The 18.6 node causes us to experience the renewed meaning of our life and a waking up to what we want to do with our lives. It involves change,including leaving home, training for a new profession or job, and new friends are cultivated. However, there is also the loss of the familiar people, experiences and places of childhood. It is also a period of great freedom where we have the capacity to shape our future destiny without the constraints of the earlier developmental issues. It is a period of grace that cushions the earlier turbulence of adolescence and provides a pathway into the adult world.

Physical development

Sexual development in adolescence provides a particularly complex challenge, which involves "the unification of sensual biological sexuality and psychological eroticism" (Lievegoed, 2003, p.40). It is important that both of these aspects awaken during adolescence. Together, they can form the bridge to adult intimacy that is so central to the next phase of development. The danger of adolescence is that if sexuality persists without the awakening of eroticism then it becomes simply a means of relating to an object of desire without the subjective intimacy and appreciation of the other person's spirit that should characterise a mature adult sexual relationship. Sexual behaviours are problematic in relation to adolescents whenever there is lack of consent, lack of equality, or coercion, either physical or manipulation, trickery, peer pressure, bribes or intimidation. Ryan (2000, p.44), after extensively reviewing the research, lists in detail normal sexual behaviours; those requiring an adult response and guidance; those requiring correction and illegal behaviours requiring immediate legal intervention as follows:

Normal:
- sexually explicit conversation with peers
- obscenities and jokes within the cultural norm
- sexual innuendo, flirting and courtship
- interest in erotica
- solitary masturbation
- hugging, kissing, holding hands
- petting, making out, fondling
- mutual masturbation
- monogamist intercourse after 16 years of age (or 17 in some states)

Requiring an adult response
- sexual preoccupation interfering with daily functioning
- pornographic interest
- promiscuity
- obscenities
- sexual graffiti impacting individuals
- embarrassment of others with sexual themes
- violation of another body space
- single occurrences of peeping or exposing

Requiring correction
- compulsive masturbation, especially chronic or public
- degradation of self or others with sexual themes
- attempting to expose others' genitals
- sexually aggressive pornography

- sexually explicit conversations with young children
- touching others genitalia
- sexually explicit threats

Illegal behaviours defined by law

- obscene phone calls, voyeurism, exhibitionism, sexual harassment
- child sexual abuse
- sexual assault
- rape
- bestiality
- genital injury to others

In addition, adolescents are today vulnerable to a wide range of sexually exploitative behaviours via the internet with promises of blind dates, chat-room liaisons and a range of other ways of meeting persons sexually interested in the meeting. Without community credentials or character references, the adolescent is playing up a blind alley and they may meet a positive caring human being or they may meet the equivalent of Jack the Ripper. The use of the internet to disseminate sexual activities, to engage in online pornography and exploitative sites remains an ongoing threat to the healthy sexual development in this phase. Delmonico and Griffin (2008, p.433) outline these hazards and give examples of online language used to create relationships sexually. These are accessible on *htttp://www. noslang.com.* Examples include:

Cybering: Engaging in sexual activity with someone online
Lurking: Non-participation in a chat room
IRL: Lets meet in real life
POS: Parent over shoulder
MOTSS: Member of the same sex

The biological changes between 12 and 16 years are profound and exceeded only by the massive physical change in the first year of life. However, in adolescence they have extensive psychological, emotional and social impacts on the adolescent who becomes "the fascinated, charmed or horrified spectator that watches the development or lack of development of adolescence" (Tanner cited in Peterson, 2010,p.302). Not only does the adolescents' height and secondary sexual characteristics such as hair and breasts mature differentially, but there are many asynchronies in their development that leave the already self-conscious adolescent reeling in shock. Particularly annoying is the rapid growth of the nose before the rest of the face. Also the oil producing glands develop more rapidly than their ducts causing facial blemishes at the time when appearance really counts. In addition, the hips and shoulders of girls do not develop in synch so that the appearance of the body is disproportionate.

The menarche or first period has a wide range of variation in girls starting as early as 10 years in some girls and as late as 16 in other girls. The average age in 2006 was 12.29 years. Body mass index is one of the strongest indicators of the timing of girls' puberty and heavier girls reach puberty earlier than average weight girls. Ballet dancers, athletes, long-distance runners are likely to have the menarche at a later age (Peterson, 2010, p.305). In addition, girls reach puberty earlier in homes where marital relationships are discordant when compared with girls from homes were marital relationships are warm and less discordant.

Girls and boys who reach puberty on the average time make an easier adjustment than girls or boys who arrive significantly later or earlier. Early maturing boys have some advantages and generally develop higher self-esteem than other boys, but early maturing girls are often self-conscious, burdened with more household responsibilities and have lower self-esteem than girls maturing on the normative schedule. Late maturing boys and girls all suffer reduced self-esteem (Peterson, 2010).

During adolescence, there is a strong connection between body image concerns and self-concept. Universally, adolescents appear to be very critical of their body image at different times during this developmental phase. Females' preoccupation with body weight and shape means the vast majority are unhappy about it. In Australia 88 per cent of females in this phase are unhappy with their weight. The influence of the media on adolescent girls' images of the right shaped women is always profound, as is the influence of significant males in the girl's life, particularly the father. It is not surprising their self-esteem plummets from age 12 and reaches its lowest point between the ages of 18 and 20 years (Robins et al, 2002).

Puberty changes also affect relationships in the family system. At the peak of pubertal growth girls' relationships with their fathers became more distant and their relationship with their mother may become characterised by angry conflict. In addition, there are more hostile conflicts between daughters and fathers than in the preceding phase of the lifespan. There is also a greater emotional distance between sons and both parents at the peak of pubertal growth, regardless of precise age (Steinberg cited in Peterson, 2010, p.315). It is helpful, as a parent, to recognise that this period is impermanent and that once the pubertal transition has been completed, relationships with parents will generally become more positive again. This transition may take some years during adolescence and may continue to be worked through in early adulthood.

Psychological: Cognitive development

There is a profound incarnation of the adolescent's "I" which brings with it formidable powers of reasoning, logic, philosophical thinking, moral reflection, insightful assessment and critical appraisal of complicated issues. This transformation is as profound as the physical changes of this period. Of course, not all adolescents make the same changes. Piaget (1970 cited in Peterson, 2010) argued that all adolescents move to abstract thinking, which he called formal operational thinking between 11 and 15 years. However, recent research in Australia by Connell et al (cited in Peterson, 2010, p. 331) showed that more than 50 per cent of Australian youth had not made the transition to abstract thinking at 15 years of age. The majority did not reach this capacity until 17-18 years. This explains the considerable stress that many adolescents experience in high school when attempting to master maths, languages and sciences that depend on formal operational thinking. It is not surprising so many high school youths give up on learning, become professional "waggers", or leave school at the earliest opportunity.

Most importantly during this phase, particularly with the development of second order thinking which is the capacity to think about how one is thinking, the adolescent starts to radically critique parents, schools, government and world issues. Coupled with the quest for truth in this age group, hypocrisy and inauthenticity are scorned and it is common for the adolescent to develop a keen sense of social justice. On the other hand, if no vision for effective change and purpose is provided the adolescent may become sarcastic and cynical about life and its purpose. This is a serious blight on the adolescent's soul and hampers the way they will manifest their spirit in their adult years in the world.

In contrast, some adolescents become overwhelmed by the problems they now perceive around them. They detach emotionally and become preoccupied with conspicuous consumption or other narcissistic pursuits. They think only of themselves. The syndrome of self-pre-occupation without clear boundaries for responsibility and respect for others has resulted in what Carr-Grieg (2006) calls "the Princess Bitch face syndrome" which he describes as:

> An instantly recognisable adolescent female who transforms almost overnight into a rebellious stranger who behaves like a responsible adult one day and a spoilt child the next.

The way through this is clear boundaries, clear negotiated rules and consequences and if possible engagement in voluntary work helping those who are much less fortunate. This may be participating with peers in "the Forty

Hour Famine", working voluntarily in an animal refuge or travelling overseas to work in volunteer programs abroad helping communities of children and adults in need*(http://www.australianvolunteers.com/)*.

The "I" or spirit of such adolescents is likely to become sidetracked by external sensory pursuits, and unless some developmental crisis occurs, it may not move to more selflessness until they have children or during their midlife crisis. Engaging adolescents in voluntary helping projects with animals, environmental repair or overseas community assistance projects is the most powerful antidote to the development of narcissism in adolescence.

Finally, there are those adolescents who are so overwhelmed by the tasks of becoming who they are in the world, that they withdraw into what is now termed depression. Such adolescents feel they lack the space or the resources to empower themselves to overcome the obstacles they experience on the way to their fulfilment and happiness in the world. Often parents' expectations, which are out of sync with the person the adolescent is becoming, play a large role in this depression. If the parent thinks the young person should be a professional– the young person just wants to become a tattoo artist– and the parent is blocking the possibility, the youth might recoil into a depressed state and do nothing. Depression can also occur because of prolonged childhood abuse, which leaves the youth feeling the world is an unsafe place in which to live. This blocks their sense of growth and the development of their spirit manifesting in the world.

Moral reasoning – which develops from the good boy, good girl thinking of the conforming primary school child – transforms into what Kohlberg described as "law and order" thinking which respects laws beyond the individual and sees them as necessary to keep the system functioning. It is only in adulthood that there is evidence of following universal human rights principles even when they contradict existing unjust national laws (Peterson, 2010, p.342).

Psychological social: Emotional development

This is the key phase in which peer groups and friendships are of crucial importance to the adolescents' psycho-emotional health. The adolescent must fulfil their own unique identity while at the same time creating bridges to peers so that life can be filled with parties, travelling and shared interests. There is a deep longing to be profoundly understood by a significant other. Even when the parent understands, the adolescent seeks it through meaningful peer relationships. Social isolation is one of the heaviest crosses for the adolescent to bear. Yet with peers, there is often bravado, a sense of having to show your lower side rather than your higher nature for fear of being excluded from the group. Music becomes the most common language for sharing and freeing feelings of intimacy and connection. (Lievegoed, 2003). In the struggle to become the adult who one really is, the adolescent struggles between setting boundaries against difference in behaviours, particularly with peers, and seeking commonness so that they can experience a sense of belonging.

The period of 14-16 years is particularly difficult because the old structures that provided meaning to the adolescent have started to crumble and the new structures of their own selfhood are not yet in place. It is a profound period of transition with all its difficulties and challenges and opportunities for growth. Often the adolescent is trapped between not knowing and the absolute certainty they do know despite never having checked out the facts. Particularly sensitive adolescents often seek escapism or regression to try to soften the challenges and uncertainties of this period, and are vulnerable to drug addiction, particularly "uppers" like marijuana, which enable the person to leave their body and the demands of this physical world for some other place. Wrong choice here can arrest the development of the self, so that the adolescent who takes drugs from 16 years to 28 years, may reach the biological age of 28 years but in terms of the psycho-emotional maturity remain suspended at 16 years. This is a high price to pay for choosing the drug pathway which arrests the development of the adolescent's selfhood and their psycho-emotional maturity.

From 18 years of age, there is the synthesis of the adolescent's will and an emerging sense of social responsibility which accompanies a pressure to find a meaningful career that connects them to the adult world. Ultimately, the adolescent can only find himself or herself in the mirror of the world, where they find a place to express who they are and are able to embrace their social destiny (Lievegoed, 2009).

It is important to realise there are two main ways of working through the phases of child and adolescent development. There are those children and adolescents who step forward confidently at every life span step and mature according to the developmental phases in a linear way. It can be demonstrated through their performances that they are on track with developmental phases.

Then there are those children and adolescents who waiver at each development phase, that tend to retreat from time to time, and who need understanding and encouraging parents to support their somewhat delayed development progress. They often show fear and lack confidence in their abilities, feeling overwhelmed by the next developmental phase. They are reticent to perform in the outer world. However, Lievegoed (2003) notes it is often these children who do very significant things in their adult lives. Their self-development and expression has a particular strength and individuality because the forces of the young person have not been spent externally earlier in the life phases. Instead, these life forces remained within themselves to nurture themselves and their incarnating spirit. They are gathering together their life forces drawn from the world of their spirit, and this process cannot be hurried. Jordan provides an excellent example of this reticent development. He was not particularly motivated to read or write when he attended school at five years of age, preferring to make buildings and play cars and trucks. He repeatedly asked to go to a school where he only had to do maths. At eight years of age, he was so stressed and distressed by the demands of school that he just wanted "to die if life was going to be that hard". His mother had to insist to his teacher that he have the opportunity to daydream and play rather than complete worksheets at school. She told the teacher she wanted a happy child at the end of the school day, not a stressed child, and was not interested in his academic performance only his wellbeing and happiness. He would play for long hours alone in imaginative games at home and when Harry Potter books arrived on the market when he was eight years old, he quickly became a good reader. When he was 11 years of age, his mother was called to the school by the teacher because he had thrown the whole of the teacher's chalk supply for the year in the bin. When asked why he had done it he replied: "All this writing we have to do...it's just too hard for me and I thought if I threw the chalk away the teacher might think of something else to do." At 13 years, after receiving his first ever school subject prize, which was for science, he refused to participate in the extension classes for good students or to apply for advanced standing in the school community that gave him special privileges. When asked why he replied: "It's too much pressure and too many expectations." At 14 years, he developed friendships with the boys undertaking apprenticeships and played the fool in language classes to entertain those boys who found language boring and incomprehensible. At that stage, his mother was bribing him with money: $10 for every language class she was not called up to the school to discuss his behaviour and penalising him $50 for every language class that she did have to report to the language teacher to discuss his unproductive participation. She had empathy for mothers of 14-year-old boys, in the seriously staid school system that had failed to give these boys living in Australia any good reason for the compulsory learning of French. While money gave him no motivation to learn French, it gave him motivation to behave in French. At 15 years of age, he hid from any limelight. He was quiet at school and worked on a farm for pocket money. He shied from having to take responsibility to reach out to the world in any major way and complained if he was expected to catch the train instead of being driven to his destination as it was all too overwhelming to navigate the train system in a city. At 16 years of age, he made a strong step forward into his adult strength. He won a place in the National Science extension program in Canberra, confidently flew interstate and became determined to be a science researcher. He announced one day he would be school dux the following year and achieve a university entry score higher than 99 out of a possible 100. He achieved his goals at 17, attended university to study an advanced science research degree, ran an extraordinary innovative project for linking university students with voluntary mentoring of children in remote rural schools and at 21 years of age was awarded a scholarship to attend Oxford University.

By 22 years, he had travelled to more than 60 different countries in the world and had become a gregarious outgoing young man. His story is a reminder to all parents that late maturity of the self and little interest in formal schooling is not necessarily worrisome. If the child has normal physiological development, especially hearing, sight and information processing, he may be inwardly working on his self-maturity at a rate he can sustain and nurturing his potential for the time when he is able to hold it with strength and step forward into positions of creativity and or leadership in the world.

Spiritual development

The core questions of one's human spirit dominate the 14 to 21 age phase: Who am I? What do I want? What can I do? These questions become more pressing with the passing of every year of this phase as the individual seeks to discover their place in the world. The exploration of these questions may be acted out by adolescents through exploring different types of dressing, hairstyles and colours, different ways of speaking and presenting themselves and seeking different types of employment and study programs. It is not uncommon for the adolescent to change ideas about what career they would like to undertake on a regular basis or to struggle to make a choice about any career option. Erikson (1968) describes this as the phase of identity formation where the core issue to be resolved is who am I? He also notes this phase is resolved by adolescents in four different ways:

1. *Identity achievement*: When, after a period of soul searching, the adolescent decides on a career that is an accurate expression of their true self and pursues training in the field and employment. This pathway,

particularly with the array of choices offered to adolescents today, is the least common resolution, although most parents prefer it.

2. *Identity moratorium:* The adolescent simply refuses to make a decision because they do not feel they have found their choice. They may then opt for exploring the world and themselves in many different ways. These include having a gap year and not studying for a particular career but just working at odd jobs, not working at all but travelling or surfing their way around the country, or simply not making a decision at all but deciding to work at random or planned jobs. Nathan is a good example of this process. He completed Year 12, certain he was not ready for study. His first job as a brickie's labourer lasted for one year. He bought a fast car and partied hard. His second job was working with a building team cleaning up after the trades people. He then decided to study and enrolled in an apprenticeship for electricians since he noticed on work sites that he was very interested in the work done by electricians. He completed his four-year apprenticeship and at 23 years of age started working for a local company as a qualified electrician. He plans to set up his own business by the time he is 28.

3. *Identity foreclosure:* Here the young person appears to have made a decision but it is not truly a result of the young person's inner soul-searching but rather something accepted from their parents, teachers or career advisors as the pathway they should pursue. This is very common and usually the young person takes some years to discover that this is not who they are but rather what they have been trained to be. Strongly authoritarian parents are often behind identity foreclosure, having mapped out a career path for their adolescent child based on their preferences rather than that of the adolescent. This may come back to haunt them because a compliant adolescent may agree only to wake up to themselves in their 30s and discover their disconnection to work and life. Such an example is the case of Joshua who was a talented maths and science high school student and graduated with prizes in several subjects. His parents insisted on engineering despite Joshua's express interest to become an ornithologist. Joshua had been greatly interested in birds since primary school and kept diaries of all the birds he had ever seen. After one year in engineering, which he hated, he transferred to law, which his parents agreed to fund. He hated law and dropped out of university. He began working as roofing tiler, and then had a series of other odd jobs until starting work in a government department in his late 20s. By his mid-30s, he was depressed, hated work and felt stuck in a rut. He now had family

commitments, so making the transition to something that gave him joy and expressed his identity was financially very difficult. This story is so common among people whose adolescence was characterised by premature identity foreclosure.

4. *Identity diffusion*: This is the least satisfactory developmental choice because the adolescent essentially does not make any decision to support their self-development but rather is washed out to sea by the tide of life, which often means premature parenting. Identity diffused adolescents are characterised by apathy, powerlessness, confusion, insecurity, boredom and an overall disinterest in life. Mollie provides an example of this type of identity diffusion. She is indigenous, stopped attending school at 14 years of age and had her first child at 15. The father is absent but she has a good family support network. However, she is bored and often resentful that she has constraints on her social life, when she would like to be free to party and enjoy her time with her peers and new boyfriend. She has no plans for her life and does not see anything past having new boyfriends in the future.

Parents play a significant role in identity formation. Authoritarian families generally promote identity foreclosure and conformity in personality development, while identity achievement and identity moratorium adolescents tend to come from families that value individuality and connectedness. Identity diffused adolescents tend to come from families where they experience parental absence or rejection (Peterson, 2010).

Developmental decisions

My adolescent who is 14 years old is having problems at school with bullying and she is becoming shy and withdrawn and says she feels depressed. Can I do anything?

Bullying is a problem that needs to be addressed at three levels: The school, the family and the individual adolescent. If one of the parents or both in the family system regularly use bullying to get what they want then this needs to be addressed as it is highly likely the bullied adolescent is influenced by models of bullying in the family. Some teachers are bullies and bully adolescents while expecting adolescents not to bully other students. Finally, it is essential to have the bullied adolescent learn skills to stop the bullying, to stand up for herself and to speak up for her needs. Detailed exercises to achieve this outcome are documented in Sherwood (2008) Chapter 7.

When should one become worried about the low amount of food that one's adolescent daughter is consuming?

Each body shape, depending on whether the bone structure is slim, medium or heavy, has an associated normal weight. Charts plotting normal, underweight and overweight can be readily obtained for each height and body shape. Signs of concern in adolescent girls following reduced food intake are fainting spells, cessation of periods, visibility of the rib cage structure on the back, hair falling out and lying about food eaten. In addition, when the adolescents' perception is dissonant with their physical weight and they insist they are fat when one can see the shape of the bones through their skin indicates a serious problem. All of these are signs that urgent action should be taken through counselling to address the eating problem.

Conclusion

In order for the "I" or the spirit of the adolescent to enter fully into the adolescent's body and start to form the mature individuality that is separate from the parents, the adolescent must face a number of core developmental tasks and these include:

1. Forming a philosophy of life that includes moral values.
2. Merging together their temperament with their personality to lay the foundations for an integrated adult pattern.
3. Accepting the sexual aspects of themselves and deciding on their gender role.
4. Relating to another person on an intimate level.
5. Choosing a position on political and social issues.
6. Forming a career identity.
7. Developing a secure sense of self including one's ethnic identity.

It is not surprising that this phase of development should feel so pressured for adolescents' parents and teachers. It is like a second birthing, this time of the adult personality. All birthing is hard labour, and at times, the pangs of labour make the mother question her capacity to endure. So at times, the adolescent feels the pain of this birthing that is neither easy nor quick. There are moments when they wish to retreat to the womb of childhood. However, when they then realise that there is newfound freedom in the adult world, they want to take wings and fly at the speed of light. It is a time of much give and take, of balancing opposites, and parents have the difficult task of holding the middle position through the process.

SUMMARY

- I am leaving the cocoon of childhood and trying to find my own wings which are not your wings.

- I need you to remind me that I am not ugly even when I feel ugly.

- I will make mistakes but I must make choices of my own so I can learn.

- I need guidance and respect, not oppressive control and condescendence.

- I need you to believe in me especially when I doubt my ability to make it in the world.

- I am searching for whom I am and I need encouragement to pursue my career goals even if they are different from yours.

- I need to spend time with my friends and I need my parents to provide some healthy structures around these social activities.

- I need opportunities to engage in activities whereby I can contribute to the wellbeing of others less fortunate than myself.

- I need inspirational models who provide me with purpose, vision and a meaning to my human life.

- I need my parents and teachers to be authentic and not ask me to do things they do not do.

- I need space and time to explore who I am in the world through work, travel, leisure and study experiences, remembering that I have until 28 to foreclose on my career identity.

REFERENCES

Bryant, W (1993) *The Veiled Pulse of Time: Life Cycles and Destiny*, NY, Lindisfarne.

Carr-Gregg, M (2006) *Princess Bitchface Syndrome*, Melbourne, Penguin.

Delmonico, D & Griffin, E (2008) Cybersex and the e-teen: What marriage and family therapists should know,*Journal of Marital and Family Therapy* 34(4) pp.431-444

Erikson, E (1968) *Identity: Youth and Crisis*,NY, Norton.

Lievegoed, B (2005) *Phases of childhood: Growing in Body, Soul and Spirit*, Edinburgh, Floris.

Lievegoed B (2003) *Phases: The Spiritual Rhythms in Adult Life*,London, Sophia Books.

O'Neil, G& O'Neil, G (1998) *The Human Life,*NY, Mercury Press.

Peterson, C (2010) *Looking Forward through the Lifespan: Developmental Psychology* Sydney, Pearson.

Robins, R; Trzesniewski, K; Tracy, J;, Gosling, S, Potter, J (2002) Global self-esteem across the life span *American Psychology and Aging*, Vol. 17(3) Sept, 2002 pp.423-434 DOI: 10.1037/0882-7974.17.3.423

Ryan, G (2000) Childhood sexuality: a decade of study. Part 1 – Research and curriculum development *Child Abuse and neglect* 24(1) pp. 33-48

Sherwood, P (2013) *Emotional Literacy for Adolescent Mental Health*: *Experiential counselling,* Melbourne, Acer.

Anyone interested in the world generally can't help being interested in young adult culture - in the music, the bands, the books, the fashions, and the way in which the young adult community develops its own language.
http://www.searchquotes.com/quotes/author/Margaret_Mahy

CHAPTER 5

Young adulthood. 21-28 years
"Exploring your passion"

Introduction

The young adult enters this phase of the lifespan with the need to experience life and all it has to offer, not with the guidance of adults but through their own adventures and with peers. They wish to understand their most confused and difficult experiences and to see the world for themselves. As Bryant (1993, p.68) so brilliantly describes the energy of this period:

> It is the time when we celebrate our liberation from the sombre introspection of adolescence and shake our tail feathers at the world.

Young adults spend prodigious amounts of their energy searching for new experiences regardless of the sacrifice and deprivations that may be involved, particularly in relation to sleep and food. Today, travel is a priority for most young adults as it is a way to experience the diversity of humanity in a very compact space and time, and with reduced costs in airfares the world is truly their oyster. In addition, changing jobs, undertaking training in a number of separate fields and not finishing courses upon discovering they are not to one's liking, is all part of the exploratory phase of early adulthood. The sun rules this phase and the following two phases because between 21 and 42 years we have the peak activity phases of the life span. A healthy adult can burn the candle at both ends of the day and still keep active and healthy despite neglected food intakes and too little sleep. After the confusion and uncertainty of adolescence, there is a sense of a direction forward, a vision that must be pursued albeit somewhat materially at this stage. There are jobs to be had, travels to be undertaken, relationships to be explored, houses, cars and possessions to be accumulated. Gender influences these choices too with males often seeing these as a series of goals or possessions to be ticked off their list. Females may be more likely to prioritise the relationship aspect of their lives, give up more time and space for the important man in her life than he would give up for her and devote more time to finding and furnishing a place to live in which she feels is a home. Generally, it is a period of overall inner optimism and hope although emotions may still seesaw. Goethe described this period in his life as: "Exulting to the heavens and distressed to death" (Lievegoed, 2003, p.51). Young adults seem compelled to eat the bittersweet fruit of this phase of first intimate relationships, first jobs and first independence in their housing and lifestyle.

Physical/cognitive development

Physical development continues during the early part of this life span phase, particularly for males, who often continue to grow in height and width. It is not uncommon for the jaw to widen in males and the shape of the face to change somewhat as physical maturity continues during the early 20s. Such physical change is less common for females, unless they have developed very late during adolescence. The brain continues to develop, enhancing the capacity for reasoning. Flexible learning and other brain function increases are also reflected in more sophisticated motor skills and sporting prowess, increased vision and hearing and the expanded capacity for learning, memory and logical assessment (Peterson, 2010). Although during this phase, the brain mass reduces somewhat, the connections are much more efficient and this improves the efficiency and flexibility of the brain and associated tasks. These changes equip the young adult with the cognitive faculties needed to embark on the challenges and problems of adult life. During this phase, drug addiction can affect the full maturity of the brain. This is so particularly with marijuana, and in later years the will is compromised in persons who have been heavy users of marihuana in their teens and 20s. During this phase, memory as a faculty is at its peak. The levels of creativity and exploration of difference are likely to be at their highest phase in all of the lifespan. Driven primarily by the feeling life, this phase is often exuberant with times of challenge and turbulence (Staley, 1997).

Psychological social: Emotional development

Falling in love is one of the developmental hallmarks of this phase of the lifespan and the prevailing attitude is to explore relationships first. Young people in this age group expect to have a number of relationships before settling down. The length of the relationship depends on a number of factors including, each of the couple's early attachment patterns with their primary caregiver, their readiness to commit to a relationship, their compatibility in character, goals and life direction, and their cultural and economic conditions of living at the time of their meeting. It is also critically important that each person has achieved emotional independence from their parents and that they have resolved their identity crisis prior to the relationship becoming long term.

Passionate love has been demonstrated to be directly connected to physiological arousal, which the person experiences and interprets as love. Research has shown this arousal can be caused by a variety of emotions including fear, anger, jealousy, frustration and the like (Traupman and Hatfield cited in Peterson, 2010). People who have had a higher number of sexual encounters are less likely to value romanticism in their intimate relationship. Erikson defines the core social-emotional task of this phase of the life span as "intimacy versus isolation", and sees intimacy involving a reorganisation of one's character and interests in order to complement the chosen partner and in order to increase shared interests and intimacy. Successfully established intimacy of mature love should not only provide an environment that nurtures both partners, but also provide a potentially nurturing environment for any children and family members that will depend on them.

When a couple marry in their early 20s, they lack life experience and have few skills or resources to deal with life's challenges. Often, especially with pregnancy, the female forgoes her career pursuits, accepts household roles and may feel trapped and isolated. During her 20s, she will often give up a great deal for the family and for her partner, but this will all come to account as the woman enters her crisis at 33 years old. Then she will demand what she needs, especially in terms of intimacy and meaning, and he will be surprised that so much was brewing within her. He feels she has changed while he has remained consistently the same and often cannot understand why she has suddenly become unhappy and demanding. Staley, citing Brothers (1993, p.87), describes the pattern of the female at home in the 20s caring for the children and the working husband and how it builds up the energy that results in the woman experiencing low self-esteem, worries about the children, their partner and their health, low moods and sometimes depression. In contrast her husband;

> worries about inflation, the possibility of war, racial violence, the energy crisis, the stock market. But their worries seldom keep them awake at nights. They feel in robust good health. They look forward to each new day and welcome its challenge. And they consider themselves happily married.

If there are no children in the relationship and both partners work, then the pattern will be somewhat different. There is a high connection between intimacy with a partner and work success. Couples who experienced their selves as securely attached in their relationship approached their work with confidence and enthusiasm and gained high levels of satisfaction from their job. Adults with an insecure attachment pattern, which was characterised by fear of intimacy, tended to immerse themselves so completely in their job that they had no energy or resources to devote to the intimate relationships or their home life. These people often had high levels of job satisfaction but low involvement in an intimate relationship. In contrast, people whose attachment was fearful and anxious in intimate relationships carried this approach into their work place and expressed low levels of satisfaction in the workplace and at home in their intimate relationships.

By 28 years, a very noticeable change is evident. The emotional spontaneity of the earlier years is replaced by an intellectual approach to the world where events are analysed with some distance and decisions are made with greater reflection and more consideration of the facts. It is often at this point the youth who has been drug addicted at adolescence and early adulthood begins to make stirrings of a desire to deal with their addiction. There is now the very strong awareness that youth with its spontaneity and energy to explore the world without long-term commitment has changed. There is a movement towards the serious business of living in the world, establishing a family, a home and earning the income necessary to complete these tasks (Lievegoed, 2003).

Spiritual development

The young adults' spirit starts to incarnate deeply into the body as not only do they enter directly into their feeling and thinking life from an internal locus, but they begin to transcend biological drives and instincts. They are driven to find their place in the world and although still very vulnerable to assessments made by other significant adults about their abilities, they are generating their own sense of role and purpose in the world (Lievegoed, 2003). Their inner life develops with power and direction given the earlier phases of the lifespan have been satisfactorily navigated and the individual starts to feel their own power and their own person in relation to the world. Of course, if a person has been on drugs or has a disturbed childhood, these phases of self-empowerment and development will be delayed to later in the life span.

The task for the female is more complicated as they are driven by a biological need to create a potential family environment and relationship that will support it earlier than males while also under pressure to find their unique spirit or pathway in the world. This conflict between her maternal roles and her employment identity roles emerges strongly in this period and continues to be a tension throughout the adult life of most females (Moers, cited in Lievegoed, 2003). Jung goes further and argues if a woman denies her feminine maternal role at this stage of her development in favour of a masculine oriented identity, her emotional life becomes brittle and by the age of 42 she is emotionally walled off from her deepest feelings and faces an almost irrecoverable task to restore her feminine feeling life.

However, for both genders, 28 years of age marks the arrival of the spirit or "I" in the human body and it is the beginning of the adult whose spirit is now fully incarnated in their body – provided the process has not been disturbed by trauma. The protective energies of childhood, with its innocence and joy, and the turbulent energies of adolescence with the many excuses for not acting in the most skilful manner, are now fully over. By this stage, most family systems have withdrawn financial support that may have extended into the 20s during prolonged studies and the young person is expected to take responsibility for their place in the world. It is an exciting time of maturity while at the same time for some young people it can be threatening and somewhat frightening. Bryant (1993) argues that at 28 years of age psychospiritual advancement is not automatic, driven by some cosmic impulse, but rather a result of our own efforts to develop our human destiny. It is as though time has run out to play around with travel, career and relationships, and this is now the time to get really serious with the business of living. One is alone in the world and must sail one's own ship to its destiny. One could say the first 21 years of one's destiny is primarily determined by one's family system; in the period of 21 to 28 years one works to discover one's destiny and from age 28 one's destiny is carried out in the world (O'Neil & O'Neil, 1998).

Developmental decisions

When should you stick with the one job and not job-hop every year or two?

The period of 21-28 years of age is still a strongly exploratory period for the young adult during which they are testing their place in the world– with or without planning– and trying to find their niche. Some young people have a career plan while others just seem to drift from one job to the next. However, diversity of experience and the search for different experiences is a characteristic of development in this phase of the life span. It is as if they are collecting tools for their toolbox so when they come to find their interest in life, they have some diverse experiences to build on. It is also common in this era for persons to move occupations frequently, even in later phases of the life span although usually the later phases have a direct career connection.

Why does my son choose wounded women for his girlfriends? They always come with heaps of problems, do not seem to have a sense of self and cling to him to solve their problems. It never works but he keeps choosing women that need to be mended.

There may be very diverse reasons for this behaviour on the part of your son. He may be modelling on the behaviours of one or both of his parents who prioritise helping persons in distress over their family needs. It may be his self-esteem is not yet fully self-sufficient and he finds being in a helping relationship a way of feeling good about himself. Maybe he confuses his career and intimate relationship aspirations. The most important thing at this age is that he gains some self-awareness of the pros and cons of this type of intimate relationship, so as he matures he can chose with better awareness of the consequences.

Money and budgeting is a real problem for my daughter. Is this normal for this age?

This is not an uncommon problem in the early phase of this part of the lifespan, especially if the young person has not had a small budget to manage previously and has lived at home and been economically dependent for a long period during their studies. However, it is important the young adult find professional help to organise their budget as soon as they become aware that it is not a one-off blip but an ongoing feature of their lives. Budget management also has something to do with personalities as some people are naturally thrifty or very cautious in spending money, while others are very generous and very unconcerned about budget constraints. However, by 28 years of age one would hope they achieve a reasonably balanced budget in their life. Otherwise this can affect adversely their intimate relationships and family.

Conclusion

The period of 21 to 28 years of age is an exciting phase of exploration and development of the young adult's spirit as it reaches out to the world to discover the possibilities that life has to offer, and to explore their potential through the early challenges of jobs, intimate relationships, travel and economic independence. It is a time of many changes and unpredictability as decisions are often made on the run as to the next adventure or possibility. However, by the end of this phase there is a new level of awareness that has a sobering effect on the young adults' previous exuberance. By 28 years of age, the realities of finding a job, providing a house and sustaining intimate relationships for building a future family descend on the young adult with powerful immediacy. The young adult now feels they must stand completely on their own feet and step forward into their mature adult destiny.

SUMMARY

- I am exploring the world and all its opportunities so don't expect me to settle down at this time.

- I am discovering what my career might be by trying out different jobs, travelling and meeting different people.

- I am exploring intimate relationships and I am not certain of what they hold.

- I am mostly not ready to make commitments to intimate relationships until after 24 years of age.

- I love to travel and explore new things and often neglect my sleep, food and health for opportunities to explore new places and experiences.

- I need to take financial responsibility for myself as soon as I have finished my training and have a job.

- I will be different to you and I will live differently.

- I will be a bit wobbly approaching my 28th year because at that time I really feel the pressure to step into my adult responsibilities in a family, occupation and in society.

- I am dominated by my feeling life during this phase so I can make spur of the moment decisions or act on sudden impulses as I am seeking to maximise my experience in the world.

- I have intense feelings not yet fully tempered by thought.

REFERENCES

Bryant, W (1993) *The Veiled Pulse of Time: Life Cycles and Destiny,* NY, Lindisfarne.

Lievegoed, B (2003) *Phases: The Spiritual Rhythms in Adult Life,* London, Sophia Books

Lievegoed, B (2005) *Phases of Childhood: Growing in Body, Soul and Spirit,* Edinburgh, Floris.

O'Neil, G& O'Neil, G (1998) *The Human Life,* NY, Mercury Press.

Peterson, C (2010) *Looking Forward through the Lifespan, Developmental Psychology,* Sydney, Pearson.

Staley, B (1997) *Tapestries: Weaving Life's Journey,* Stroud, Hawthorn press.

One can live magnificently in this world, if one knows how to work and how to love.

— Leo Tolstoy

CHAPTER 6

Adulthood 28-35 years
"Taking charge"

Introduction

The 28 to 35-year period heralds a number of key psychological challenges and changes. We remain profoundly influenced at this stage by the sun causing us to be at the peak of our activity in the world. At this stage, we are the generators of creativity, new life and new directions. After having expanded our horizons in the previous life span phase, life is now calling us to "settle down" and choose a direction we can follow based on our experiences. It is the time to generate the lifestyle we desire. The 29th year is profound because we come under the destiny life-cycle pattern governed by Saturn which is a 30-year cycle and which essentially demands us to make decisions that will profoundly shape the next 29 years. Bryant (1993,p.118) diagrammatically represents this pattern below demonstrating how all the activity of the early stages of the 21-28 year cycle is followed by the digestion of the experiences in the second stage of the cycle, culminating in the 30-year breakthrough.

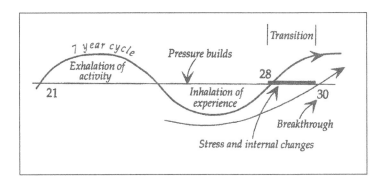

Usually the lead up to these cycles is marked by conflict, frustration and disappointment and an urgency to achieve certain developmental milestones, such as a career that one feels is satisfying, a relationship that has the potential for long-term commitment and possibly a family and a home of one's own. The 30-year landmark often heralds a release or change from the tensions of the first 30 years of our lives. The 30th year will often be an unsettling year demanding that we move forward into an uncertain future. Bryant (1993, p.105) describes this energy well as: "Storms that come to tear us down should bring about a new and finer reconstruction." This transition phase can also be marked by travel, deep reflection on one's life and a change of direction, either literally or metaphorically. Conflict, constriction, release and breakthrough readily describe this period leading up to and culminating in the 30th and 60th years. Bryant (1993, p.117) summarises the changing energies at these points in time:

> It could be described as a period of psychic congestion, a contraction prior to a burst of expansion...a concentrated transition.

They are also important years in setting one's destiny in place for future career and family patterns. Decisions made in this year usually profoundly affect us for the next 30 years at least. We also feel more pressured. At some level we must now rely on our own inner resources.

Physical development

When we arrive at 30 years of age we become aware that we have now started to move ever so slightly past our prime physical prowess of our 20s. Women tend to start to gain weight more easily and lose their youthful figures, particularly if they have had children. Men on the other hand notice that while they can still accomplish the physical challenges and tasks in their life, it takes just a little more effort than in their 20s. Athletes that continue into their 30s must work harder to keep the same form.

Psychological: Cognitive development

During this period of development, there is a strong development of thinking, particularly in relationship to reflective analytical and organisational thinking. Living day to day is no longer satisfying. We want to have a long-term plan for our life, and we want to develop roots that give our life a sense of stability. Whatever is missing we yearn for, whether it be a satisfying career, a long-term intimate relationship, a family of our own or a house of our own. The list is endless but the priorities are the missing pieces of what we believe are the jigsaw puzzle of our life. The quality of our self and other awareness becomes more penetrating, more analytical, and more skilful. The emotional enmeshment in the 20s is no longer the governing force in the psyche. In the 30s, we become much more analytical and discerning in our decision-making. We now have a bank of life experience upon which to draw and upon which to build skilful decisions as we move through our lives (Bryant, 1993). We make more reflective decisions, which are less imbued with the passion and idealism that has driven the 20s. Staley (1997, p.119) summarises this change powerfully:

> People over 30 are not as quick to risk their jobs or their families for ideals: They seem more subdued, less reckless.

Levenson (Staley, 1997, p.119) describes this as the onward and upward phase of career, particularly for men who see it as the make or break time in their career development. He is driven profoundly by his need for achievement and recognition in the world:

> If I'm not making six figures by the time I'm 40, I've had it...if I am not executive vice-president by the time I'm 35, I've had it. If I do not have a house by the time I am 30...

The competition and drive to get to the top of the hierarchy during the 30s is very strong for men. In contrast for most women, this is not so important as they seek more rounded fulfilment that balances their family, career and partner needs.

Psychological social: Emotional development

The 30th year is a time for major reappraisal of self and reappraisal of our current life projects and directions. This may produce tension and lead us into conflict in our career or relationships particularly if they are not compatible with whom we are becoming in our full adult self. Bryant, (1993, p.104) also points out that our decisions in our 30th year are often ones that are linked to the broader social and political environment in which we live as this year has a way of interweaving our personal and social destiny. Many of an individual's significant deeds or actions in their life are launched between 29 and 30 years. The Buddha began his teaching at 29 years, Mahavira, the founder of Jainism, and Christ began their public teaching at 30 years. Winston Churchill left the Tory party and joined the Liberals in his 30th year and the great general Hannibal began his audacious campaign to cross the Alps and attack Rome in his 30th year.

During the 30s, it is easy to take on too many financial and material responsibilities as we are caught in the energy of competition, acquisition and promotional opportunities. We may ignore or override our deeper longings at this stage because we leave little or no time to reflect on ourselves. Life is very full, too busy and too outwardly focused.

This is particularly problematic in the area of relationships. It is likely that an intimate relationship will start to lose it shine and dazzle by the 30s and intimacy resolves into a practical routine that constitutes daily life, the mortgage and in many cases, children as well. The man is often most engaged in the outer world of work and does not notice the inner changes that the woman is unable to avoid noticing. Around 32-33 years of age, a woman starts to become acutely aware of her emerging personality and her need for intimacy of a deeper nature in her work, her relationships and her life. She wants to become more fully who she is and often she expresses this as emotional dissatisfaction with the status quo. She begins to complain to her partner that she is not satisfied in the amount of time they spend together, or the amount of his presence and attention in their relationship. Her awareness of her deepening self-consciousness can challenge a relationship deeply, and either the couple rise to the new growth impetus and renew their commitment and intimacy at a different level, or there is a strong possibility that the relationship will breakdown.

Alternatively, the couple may try to resolve the tension by not taking responsibility for their own role in the relationship and the need to develop their character. Instead, they will ignore this psycho-emotional task of the 30s and project the task onto yet another partner. Affairs may develop with the man who is usually looking for a younger woman to adore him so he does not have to face changing himself and can still feel secure. The woman seeks affairs with a man to feel that she is still attractive instead of developing her inner self-esteem. Alternatively, she may rely on her husband to provide her sense of self-esteem. Both of these roads usually end in suffering, disappointment and betrayal for one or more persons, and the essentially psycho-emotional task of working with one's imperfections and weaknesses of character to become a stronger human being is avoided. These tasks must be confronted and if they are not, they will return in the 40s with a vengeance and then they will wreak havoc in the individual's life. It is important to recognise that at this stage, the quality of a marriage or relationship reflects the quality of the inner work each person is willing to do on their own inadequacies and to work to meet these needs and not to expect their partner to meet these needs and make them happy. The sobering lesson of the 30s is to realise, albeit slowly for most people, that one is responsible for one's own happiness.

Those persons not in an intimate relationship feel the pressure to find one, but it is more difficult than in the 20s because we are more aware of our own and others' limitations. We also have a clearer sense of our needs and our incompatibilities with a range of potential partners. We are also more wary of potential partners with "baggage" which can include an ex-partner, children from a previous marriage, careers that involve extensive travel and illnesses that are prolonged. Unlike in our 20s, when we were prepared to give most potential partners a chance, we now evaluate critically the potential of the relationship in terms of our experience and our sense of its compatibility.

Spiritual development

During this period the "I", or the sense of our own spirit and destiny, enters deeply into our thinking faculties and characteristics of "I" presence in our lives are focus, organisation, memory and goals (Staley, 1997). These strongly characterise this phase as the "I" expresses itself through thinking in particular, and our lives take on a new shape and a new pattern. We organise them to achieve our career and family aspirations with a vigour and commitment not previously evident in the life span.

The downside is that as we become more aware of self and others through our thinking faculties – as they are more strongly penetrated by our "I"– we develop higher levels of insight. We can also become quite judgmental, critical, cold in our thinking of others and contemptuous of situations and people who do not meet our standards. This can lead to dissatisfaction with others and ourselves, an inner malaise that cannot be solved by thinking alone and which will rear its head in our 40s. Excessive criticism and judgment leads to disconnection from others and from the world and can result in either self-righteousness or narcissism, neither of which promotes healthy development of the human spirit. Our increasing awareness of self and others demands we make the effort to develop empathy and understanding for those who are different to ourselves if we are to continue to mature spiritually and morally (Staley, 1997).

Also during this phase of the life span – with its challenge in relationships, careers and family building– we learn the limits of our thinking to solve all our problems. We cannot organise and plan ourselves through many of life's challenges. This recognition, however gradual, awakens within us the need to expand our feelings and explore further our human capacities to problem solve as we move into the next phase of the life span.

Developmental decisions

As a woman, what can I do to make the 33rd year less stressful in terms of my intimate relationships?

Develop intimacy with yourself and commit yourself to working to understand yourself better and to strengthen yourself so you do more of the things you love in your life. Remember, he is not responsible for your happiness, only you can make yourself happy. When you speak up to your partner about your desire to share more intimately it is important it is done without blame or accusation.

Conclusion

By 35 years, we have developed a more realistic picture of who we are and dropped many of the illusions that coloured our earlier portraits of ourselves. Likewise, our judgment of other persons is also markedly more realistic and more accurate. We are at the peak of the arc of our productivity in the workplace and carry the responsibilities of work, family and community engagements. It is a hectic period driven by the will, often with inadequate time for our own lives. We are the wheels of the lifespan carrying the primary responsibilities for children, work and society at a level not often exceeded in any other phase of the life span.

SUMMARY

- I know how I want to organise my world and I have plans.

- I can be very judgmental of others who do not act and behave in ways that I approve and I can be quite self-righteous about my views.

- I am finding intimate relationships becoming quite routine and at times more challenging.

- Work and raising a family are my primary commitments often to the exclusion of my own wellbeing.

- I am not at my most tolerant phase of the lifespan so you need to understand that I am often very certain about many things.

- If I am a woman, I am vulnerable at 33 years and need more intimacy. I feel alone in the world and I will make new demands for intimacy in my relationships.

- I feel I am responsible for those younger and those older than myself.

- I become stressed if I think I am missing out on a family, relationships, a family home or the type of work I would like.

- If I am a man, I am likely to be pushing myself to get to the top of the ladder as quickly as possible.

- If I am a woman, I am likely to want to start a family in this phase if I have not already begun in my 20s. It will become increasingly urgent as I approach 40.

REFERENCES

Bryant, W (1993) *The Veiled Pulse of Time: Life Cycles and Destiny,* NY, Lindisfarne.

Lievegoed, B (2003) *Phases: The Spiritual Rhythms in Adult Life,* London, Sophia books.

O'Neil, G& O'Neil, G (1998) *The Human Life,*NY, Mercury Press.

Peterson, C (2010) *Looking Forward Through the Lifespan: Developmental Psychology,*Sydney: Pearson.

Staley, B (1997) *Tapestries: Weaving Life's Journey,* Stroud, Hawthorn Press.

Your family and your love must be cultivated like a garden. Time, effort and imagination must be summoned constantly to keep any relationship flourishing and growing.

—Jim Rohn

http://quotations.about.com/od/famousquotes/a/famousfamily.htm

CHAPTER 7

Mature Adulthood 35-42 years "Reviewing the life plan"

Introduction

The sun is still governing this phase and the demands to perform in the world through work, family and community are still central to this period of what Erikson describes as "generativity". However, the sun's energies that have governed the life since the age of 21 are beginning to wane. Lievegoed (2005, p.196) describes the transition to this phase succinctly and powerfully. It is the phase of the will:

> From the age of 20, I learned about life by throwing myself into it, and from the age of 30, I consolidated and structured this experience, but what do I do with the experience now?

This is truly the time for realism, for downsizing the dreams to fit the day-to-day realities of life. There is a clear knowledge of what one feels capable of, although this is less so for women who have devoted much of their 30s to child rearing. However, it is the period in which questions arise about the life plan that was so certain in the 30s. Questions arise, often semi-consciously, as niggling doubts but which gradually accumulate. Is this really the career I want in my life? Is this all there is to life? Is my relationship still alive or is it just a routine? Would a holiday pick me up? The list of questioning which starts in this period tends to grow in the 40s into a book that demands to be read and resolved.

In this phase of the life span, we are still in a cycle of expansion. We remain much more interested in the present and the future and show little interest in the past. While we are becoming aware of the gap between the reality of our actual performance, our achievements and our expectations, we are not unduly disturbed by its presence. We still feel that we have the power to shape our lives. However, at this time the single most important event is the emerging of the self as a spiritual being. This starts to stir within us, demanding our higher-order values and needs are acknowledged. At 35, 37-38 and at 42, the interior demands for change press upwards and disturb our routine day-to-day life. This occurs at first with questions and doubts but on occasions there may be an eruption through a crisis of health or family that forces us to review and reappraise our values and direction in life (Bryant, 1993).

Physical development

A number of physical changes start to herald the decline of the physical body after 35 years of age. From 35,the maximum oxygen intake declines by about one per cent per year. The thymus gland decreases in size and T-cell functioning, which governs immunity, also begins to decline. The quality of the female reproductive system also declines and there is increased risk of congenital deformities, particularly chromosome related disorders in development such as Down's syndrome. There is a gradual decline in skin elasticity, particularly in areas that have been exposed to the sun. From 40 years of age, eyesight begins a slow decline as does smell and taste. Tastebuds decrease in number and sensitivity. From 40 years of age, there is also a decrease in the elasticity of the blood vessels, which will affect systolic blood pressure (Peterson, 2010,p.420).

Physical injuries and recovery after 40 are profoundly affected by the ageing process. For example, recovery from the same brain injury is most rapid in childhood, then adolescence and early adulthood. It slows down in middle adulthood and declines rapidly with ageing (Peterson, 2010, p.420).

Psychological: Cognitive development

The first growth spurt in adulthood occurs between 18 years and the early 20s. The second very significant spurt in brain growth occurs between 25years of age and 40 years. This phase focuses primarily on the frontal lobes of the brain, which is the place of "insight" or the non-impulsive mind consciousness. It also includes the limbic system and the neural connections deep within the brain. These parts of brain development form the foundation for the mature cognitive powers of middle and later adulthood, which are characterised by insight, reflectiveness and the capacity to develop broad goals and plans that embrace significant different interests. The adult brain remains responsive to new challenges, and gains in brain structure and complexity can arise particularly if a person specialises in certain activities that use particular parts of the brain. For example,a London taxi cab study showed that experienced taxi drivers had a larger posterior hippocampus region in their brains with many more neural connections than the average person of the same age, and this is the part of the brain where spatial representations and maps of localities are stored. What you do and how you do it profoundly affects which parts of the brain continue to develop in these adult years (Peterson, 2010, p.421).

There is also considerable evidence that different parts of the brain develop differently based on gender differences, but whether culture and experience causes the differences or gender factors alone is still in debate. Males do score higher on performances relating to mathematics, geometry, physical aggression, justice, reasoning, willingness to have casual sex and throwing speed. Females on the other hand score highest in relation to communication skills, particularly self-disclosure, smiling and depression (Peterson, 2010, p, 423).

Psychological social: Emotional development

Roberts and Del Vecchio (2000) noted that in large population samples personality growth in adulthood is considerably more stable than in childhood. In particular, the traits of extroversion, cheerfulness, conscientiousness, neuroticism and openness to experiences remain relatively stable after the 40s (Peterson, 2010, p.424).

However, at an emotional level, a new energy is arising because of the 37-year moon node which profoundly affects the emotional life. The 37.2 node often follows a period of loss of stamina for one's profession, loss of interest in what had been one's preceding occupation and a search for something to revitalise life which perhaps is a new direction or a new purpose. Women who have not yet had children at this age, may reconsider and decide to have a child if other circumstances are favourable. Something stirs within us at this time to move us towards finding a new way to connect with our life purpose and the destiny of our spirit or highest potential in the world. It is the beginning of the stirrings of reviewing the values that we thought were so clear in the first part of the 30s and reassessing what is giving us satsifaction and fulfillment. The challenges of the 30s can start to become "old hat" by the 40s. One now reflects on how one can live one's life differently, or do one's work in a new way with different values and goals. Relationships are also beginning to demand fresh energy if they are to be sustained into the 40s. It is a time of uncertainty and reappraisal (Lievegoed, 2003,p.64).

This is the time in which we start to reappraise work and the use of one's productive energies so as to benefit not just oneself and one's family but to contribute to the wellbeing of society as a whole. Havinghurst (Peterson, 2010,p.444) describes the key values and behaviours in this transition to the 40s as activism, altruism and mentoring. The need is to reach out to society and to the community and to connect to values beyond one's self-preoccupation. One needs to find connections and meaning in wider community networks. It is here that volunteering can become very signficiant, whether it is becoming secretary for the local sports club, engaging in a community tree planting association or a community progress association, or assisting in fund raising for disadvantaged groups in society.

Spiritual development

Traditionally, 35 years is viewed as the midpoint in the lifecycle. The first 35 years are devoted to manifesting and working on the external world. However, at 35 years, there are the beginnings of the stirrings of working on the inner self–improving the quality of the inner life within ourselves. Steiner argues that spiritually, a human spirit with its potential for the manifestation of wisdom is only really liberated from 35 years of age. Only then can a person start to give advice based on their reflection of their experiences in the world. It is also the age at which the spiritual forces within an individual that bring about wisdom are released. Knowledge alone will not satisfy the individual's deepest yearnings, which are for self-realisation of the knowledge in the form of wisdom. (O'Neil and O'Neil, 1998, p.34).

It is during this period that the intellectual certainty of the early 30s starts to give way to the demand for deeper meaning and the search for something of more lasting value. It is here the spiritual needs of the human spirit start to raise their hands. They will be next in the queue for attention, and although at this time only their stirrings may be felt, these spiritual yearnings are the beginning of an avalanche that will confront the person from 42 years onwards. After having confronted the challenges of the world and created a plan for dealing with them in the early 30s, a completely new dimension of existence starts to dawn upon the individual. This is the challenge to carve one's deepest values onto the face of one's life. Nothing less will be satisfying. The life forces that to this stage have been preoccupied with perfecting the physical development of the human being are now released for the development of wisdom and knowledge that is truly owned through work at the anvil of one's own soul experiences in the world.

The astral or instinctive forces that so strongly governed the teens, 20s and early 30s, now begin to recede. As they recede the higher consciousness, the "I" or insightful spirit of a human being starts to dominate the human life span (O'Neil and O'Neil, 1998). The opportunities of human life will demand that from 35 years onward the decision making gradually reflects more and more depth of self-awareness, self-ownership and self-maturity. It is at this time that one is more able to detach from a rigid set of values and judgments and to reflect with more awareness and clarity on the possibilities of human experience and existence.

Developmental decisions

Why does the 37th year often result in new directions?

Not only are we influenced by the sun activity but also by the 18.6-year rhythms that are governed by the moon and which release considerable energy for new directions, changes and a new awareness. The moon rhythms influencing us are 18.6-year rhythms which occur at the following ages, 18.6, 37.2, 55.8 and 74.4 years, and at this time there is considerable energy released for change and new awakenings. For change to occur there is often a preceding ending or death that opens up new directions in our lives. The moon node periods often follow a trauma – either a physical illness, loss of a loved one, an employment crisis, or some other transitionary event. For women who have not yet had children, this year may also raise the issue of having children, now or never. It can also be a period of ending of old intimate relationships and the starting of a new intimate relationship.

I don't have the same energy for life that I once had. is there something wrong here?

Eliminating any possible physical disease, it is quite normal for the etheric body or life force to start naturally declining from around 40-42 years. This is usually noticed first by a drop in our energy levels and the emerging awareness that we do not quite have the stamina we had in our 30s to overcome nights without sleep and prolonged physical exertions. This is part of normal development and accelerates as we enter our 40s. It becomes essential that we eat well, exercise and sleep well in order to maintain our vitality levels. These issues are of much less concern for most people in their 30s.

Conclusion

This period is characterised by inner changes in the relationship to oneself. Our old patterned methods of thinking and approaching the world are becoming unsatisfactory as our deeper self demands a louder and stronger voice in our life. The self-observer who is none other than oneself senses there is more to life than previously concluded. This is a dual edged sword, which on the one hand stirs up doubts and discord within our deepest self but which on the other hand cuts a new pathway through to personal growth and development. This transition always occurs although with a different force in the life of different personalities. It is subtle and gentle for some people, and overt and forceful for others. It is summed up as follows:

> The 35th year of life is an important boundary. There man crosses, so to speak, a bridge. There the world he came out of withdraws, and from within he gives birth to a new world. (O'Neil and O'Neil, 1998, p.40).

Awakening consciousness drives us with both its strength and new direction and its emptiness and loneliness. The routine of life no longer brings the same contentment, nor do the physical pleasures of the world give us the same level of satisfaction. We are forced to forge a new sense of value, meaning and direction that emanates from our human spirit which can provide the spiritual energy for the future years as our physical energy starts to fade (Staley,1997). It is the only way forward to a productive, energetic, creative and inspiring second half of life.

SUMMARY

- I am moving from focusing on the outer world and goals to focusing on my inner experience and shaping the world accordingly.
- I am modifying my goals in the world to reflect my new values and insights.
- I am no longer shackled by the constraints of the development of my physical body or my emotional life and I have released this energy to cultivate insights based on my experience.
- I am becoming free to provide leadership in my community.
- I am able to share my experience to inspire others.
- I am moving from the world others have created for me to a new world that I am creating for myself out of my experience.
- I can be responsible for my own happiness.

- I begin to loosen my judgments about others and become more open to different ways of being in the world.
- I am becoming more conscious of myself and my unique needs.
- I will face crisis to force me to step up to my full human potential.

REFERENCES

Bryant, W (1993) *The Veiled Pulse of Time: Life Cycles and Destiny,* NY, Lindisfarne.

Lievegoed, B (2003) *Phases: The Spiritual Rhythms in Adult Life,* London, Sophia Books

Peterson, C (2010) *Looking Forward Through the Lifespan: Developmental Psychology.* Sydney, Pearson.

Staley, B (1997) *Tapestries: Weaving Life's Journey,* Stroud, Hawthorn Press.

Most younger adults anticipate that between their late thirties and their early fifties a day will come when they suddenly realize that they have squandered their lives and betrayed their dreams. They will collapse into a poorly defined state that used to be called a nervous breakdown. Escape from this black hole will mean either embracing an un-American philosophy of eschatological resignation or starting over – jaded stockbrokers off to help Mother Teresa, phlegmatic spouses off to the StairMaster and the singles scene. In short, they will have a midlife crisis.

—"Midlife Myths" by Winifred Gallagher in The Atlantic, May 1993

CHAPTER 8

Middle Age: 42-49 years
"Resolving the unresolved"

Introduction

We have all heard of the midlife crisis, so most of us arrive with some uneasy feelings in relation to this age. We have heard of friends and relatives who have either imploded and become sick physically or mentally, or exploded and taken off in a new sports car with someone half their age to the Caribbean Islands. Midlife crisis is a term coined in 1965 by Elliott Jaques to describe the life-span period where adults come to realise there is limited time left in their life, their own mortality and the limitations on their abilities to achieve what they wish to achieve. It can be triggered by a crisis relating to health, family or work and the result is the need to make significant changes in career, work-life balance, marriage, romantic relationships, expenditures or physical appearance. Dante (Bryant, 1993, p.79) described this phase as the "dark wood":

> midway through this way of life we're bound upon, I woke to find myself in a dark wood. Where the right road was wholly lost and gone.

On the upside, this phase of the lifespan is a breakthrough to personal renewal, fresh opportunities and new directions. It can be the period in our life where we discover other aspects of ourselves that we have not previously mobilised. Our creativity may have been repressed by our conformity to societal norms, our feeling life may have been strangled by the intellectual milieu in which we have trained and worked, and our sense of the spiritual may have been suffocated by our focus on material possessions. Now is the opportunity to bring our hidden qualities out of the cupboard and into the light. Now is the time to begin to rethink the whole of who we are, not just those specialised aspects of ourselves that have worked well to negotiate the education and employment systems in which we have previously been engaged.

This middle-age phase is the stage for self-discovery and calls for a new play to be performed on the stage of our lives. The intensity of the turbulence, change and distress in this phase depends on how much we engage with our spirit in rethinking and remoulding the 35-42 phase of the lifespan, and how much unprocessed material we bring to this stage from earlier phases in the lifespan. Like a train fully loaded with carriages from previous phases of the lifespan, we hit the peak of the upward rise of the hill at 42 years of age. Thereafter it is downhill all the way. If the carriages are laden with unresolved traumas and broken relationships, unresolved grief and loss, then the down-hill ride may well be characterised by some derailment, an accident or an illness here or there as the stress of trying to keep the overburdened train on the tracks is simply too much. We are confronted with the need to download our excess cargo and this often requires us to access new skills and new parts of ourselves that have previously lain dormant but which are essential for our journey forward into the next phases of the lifespan.

Middle age forces us to look inward, to take the mirror of self-reflection and use it to develop greater insight. We do not always like what we see and too often we realise that parts of ourselves are numbed, stunted or withered from disuse. In the back of our mind a critical question is surfacing:

> Have we, in the struggle with our daily responsibilities, blighted our potential by discarding our once all-important ideals? Those of us who have earned no spiritual income for years have nothing put aside for these rainy days. Our comfortable life-styles, like our convictions, may have hardened into concrete strait-jackets(Bryant, 1993,p.81).

In the face of our dissolving sense of self, certainty and happiness, there is usually a series of unresolved issues. A boring job which has become routine and unsatisfactory, a relationship that has lost its passion and intimacy, and communication has become superficial. The spontaneity and enthusiasm in the family life has disappeared amid the demands of children, work and mortgages. The children have often outgrown the family and as adolescents spend little time at home. The home is now reduced to two persons and the warmth and presence that children added to the household is now gone. The empty nest is no longer a place of vitality but rather a shadow of its former warmth and energy.

Rather than face this emptiness, some individuals choose to flee through drugs, return to adolescent behaviours or begin a series of marital affairs, often with younger partners. These escapes will not fulfill the demands of this phase of the lifespan. Here one is called to create more solid ground that is truly one's own and not built upon or around one's children or partner. Instead, the individual must face that they are standing on shifting sands and they face a future of the ageing process that requires grit, guts and grace to navigate.

Physical changes

This is the start of the involution of all the tissues in the body. The most common example is the hardening of the tissue of the eye, leading to difficulty when focusing on reading and leading most people who work at close range to seek help with prescription glasses. This is accompanied by the decline in the endocrine glands in both men and women and the shift in the hormonal balance, which is maintained by the organs of internal secretion.

Menopause is the major sign of this phase. It begins anywhere from the late 30s and culminates at any time up to 55 years, the average age being 51 years. It is a gradual process with oestrogen levels dropping throughout the 40s that results in substantially reduced fertility and the final cessation of fertility. This process for some women can be associated with irritability, insomnia, reduced sexual drive, hot flushes, migraines and weight gain. There is no evidence to link menopause with any mental health problems in women (Peterson, 2010). In their 40s, men experience a decline in testosterone, lowering of sperm count and a reduction in sexual drive. These physical changes often complicate the cognitive and emotional changes that are also occurring at the same phase in the life span. It can be difficult to distinguish what is solely an emotional problem and what is a sexual problem. These two are interwoven.

In the anthroposophical model of a human being, we would say that during menopause the astral forces, which carry the sexual forces, are no longer required in reproduction. They are released from the womb area and can be used by the woman cognitively and emotionally to create her presence in the world. She now has an increased amount of physical energy to shape her place in the world and fully express her personhood. The successful transition of the 40s demands that a woman find her place in the world and has the opportunity to make her mark on the world.

Men also are affected by a decline in sexual prowess that can be masked by an increased desire for sex. The physical symptoms of male menopause can include attacks of palpitations as well as emotional instability and emotional moodiness, with feelings of helplessness, powerlessness and vulnerability (Lievegoed, 2003). Often in counselling, men will tell you they feel, for the first time in their marriage, that they are more emotionally vulnerable than their wives. They will admit that she needed them when she was younger, but now they need her more than she needs them.

Psychological: Cognitive development

Cognitive growth continues but it is contingent on the regular application and development of expertise in particular areas of work or home life. Persons who consistently engage in particular types of cognitive activities show higher levels of problem solving abilities in these areas than individuals who do not. The core developmental stimulus at this stage is activity. Those parts of the brain actively engaged in your life continue to develop. In particular, some higher order post-formal cognitive thinking develops. These skills are contextually valid thinking and specialised reasoning that solves specialised problems in their workplace. The development of dialectical thinking increases in this age group. It is the capacity to perceive fundamental contradictions in everyday dilemmas and to discover higher-order synthesis to apply to dynamic and changing problems. Arlin (1990) discovered that generating multiple new solutions to routine or new problems escalated in this period (Peterson, 2010, p.427).

Psychological: Social-emotional development

There are significant social-emotional challenges in this phase of the life span. Extensive research across different cultures has shown that the U-curve of marital happiness illustrated below, reflects the normative marriage development cycle. The lowest part of the curve, which includes child rearing and the launching of children coincides with low satisfaction. Often the 40s represent the culmination of these phases of the marriage cycle. Interestingly, after children leave home, the wives' satisfaction goes up considerably while the husbands' satisfaction goes down considerably. Women now see themselves as free to explore the world and are often unavailable for home duties. The husband now finds the home is no longer the centre of her world and he may find himself washing his own clothes and cooking some of his own meals.

It is significant that although women's satisfaction escalates rapidly after the launching of the children, male satisfaction continues to decline. For many women, this becomes a period in which they can launch themselves into the world and pursue the aspirations and interests that have been deferred during child raising and they feel a new space and freedom to seek the fulfilment of their destiny. Riding the Mars energy of this period, which promotes activity in the world, these women can find satisfaction as they submerge themselves in newfound careers and pursuits in the world. In contrast, men are often seeking relief from the endless grind of the workplace, seeking to change their lives in new ways that are more creative. Men often feel stuck

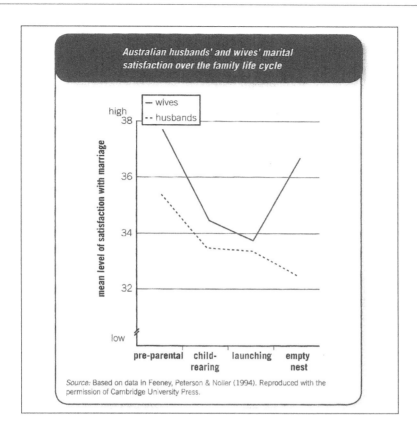

Australian husbands' and wives' marital satisfaction over the family life cycle

Source: Based on data in Feeney, Peterson & Noller (1994). Reproduced with the permission of Cambridge University Press.

because in many cases change would involve retraining and substantial income reductions for their family. Too many men are socialised to believe they must keep earning big incomes or they are a failure. The reality is many men at this phase would do well to reduce their incomes in favour of more creative hobbies or more engaging work.

Jung points out that at this point in the life cycle the majority of women move from being dominated by the feminine qualities of their psyche, which he terms the anima, to being dominated more by the previously suppressed masculine qualities of their psyche, which he calls the animus. The qualities of anima are nurturing, cooperation, creativity, softness, intuition and human relationships, while the qualities of animus are competition, action in the world, logic, rationality, structure, organisation, object relationship and competition. Men, in contrast, need to move away from being dominated by their animus and bring their suppressed anima to the fore, and they need to engage in activities and occupations that embrace the qualities of anima. This is culturally and socially very challenging for men but if they fail to make this transition, they often end up moody, bitter or resentful. This period is challenging also for women as it demands that both men and women take back their projections and expectations that they have placed on each other. For example, generally a woman will expect a man to embody all the male qualities of animus and a man will expect his wife to embody all the female qualities of anima. Both can become critical of each other when they fail. The challenge of this period is to withdraw the projections and take ownership of developing the opposite qualities yourself.

Generally, this means women must develop qualities that are more masculine and men must develop qualities that are more feminine (Shealy, 1976). Essentially, this is the period of the crossing of the genders in opposite directions. It can be succinctly summarised as follows: "For the first 20 years of the marriage she waits for him to come home to dinner, but for the next 20 years of the marriage he waits for her to come home to dinner." It is one of the most challenging times in couple relationships in the entire lifespan. This period lacks the passion and vitality of the early years of the relationship. Furthermore, this period has not yet reached and achieved the stable companionship of the later years of the marriage cycle. During this midlife crisis in relationships– as in the first two years of a relationship– divorces are most common.

A number of factors have been found to foster marital happiness in this phase of the life span and these include personal growth and personality development, unpaid leisure pursuits, cultural interests that are shared and shared travel. New experiences between the couple must be cultivated and new bonds and interests created. Often, decline in income that results from the husband spending increasing time with his wife and family can increase marital happiness. In addition, satisfying self-disclosure among couples as well as sharing positive moments contributes greatly to couple satisfaction(Peterson, 2010).

Spiritual development

This phase of the life span has as its core psycho-spiritual challenge what Erikson terms "generativity" that involves a creative contribution to the world. This is achieved through parenthood, but can be achieved in a variety of other ways including altruistic volunteer work, work in the human services, or other work where individuals experience themselves as contributing to the world in which they live. Stagnation is the consequence of failed generativity and here the individual feels stuck, worn down, unmotivated and uninspired to continue with their life. Chronic fatigue or another debilitating illness is quite common when the individual reaches this point. Women are most likely to develop a mental health problem such as depression, but it is also common among men in this phase of the lifespan when life seems to lose its purpose and direction.

O'Connell (1981) cites Jung as likening this phase of the life span to a "creative illness" which calls for a renewal of the creative spirit within us in order to recover. It is the period that Jung describes as "freeing oneself from ego imprisonment" (Lievegoed, 2003, p.74). Bryant (1993, p.83) describes it as follows:

> Middle age challenges us to disperse the shadow of our psychological past, which includes all the character weaknesses and imperfections imprinted in our youth and reinforced throughout the years. It is a time for change, for self-examination and self-acceptance, a time for truth...

However, the promise is of a rejuvenation of our human spirit and a new pathway carved out for the individual to tread that is ultimately more satisfying than the old pathway. Yet at the time it rather feels like one is being battered by the winds and is lost in the "dark wood". One feels as though one is wrestling with the meaning of it all, facing the emptiness and searching for new signposts. Some attempt to avoid this journey through addictions, consumerism, travel, virtual realities or affairs but this will compromise greatly the quality of the future phases of the life span because the human spirit cannot be tricked out of its destiny. This is a fatal mistake for it is the preparatory transition for the liberation of our higher spiritual being towards greater insight and wisdom. It is a period that is calling us to experience greater liberation from the old routines of body and mind and to become acquainted more fully with our unique human spirit that will drive our destiny to greater heights of satisfaction and fulfilment.

Developmental decisions

My husband is moody and irritable. What is the best response I can make to support him?

The greatest deed you can do for him is not to react back with anger, criticism or judgment. In relationships, if one person can balance the ship, it usually stays afloat. If both persons enter the fray then the ship is in danger of sinking. Encourage him to try out new hobbies and experience things he has only dreamed about. Affirm to him that you are happy with less material things so that he has the space and time to find a change in his work that he will find more satisfying. Encourage him to find his creative self and to pursue interests that are focused on the more feminine qualities of care, human relationships, cooperation and creativity. Remember, only he can make himself happy and you are not responsible for his happiness. You are responsible for your own happiness and maintaining your own peace and equilibrium.

My wife is becoming depressed with the children leaving. How can I best support her?

Encourage her to develop interests in the world. Joining a group of people who are engaged in some sort of physical activity – whether walking or gym – is very helpful if one is feeling depressed. Encourage her to branch out on a new pathway, explore new interests and take up a study course in an area of her interest. Remind her that this is the beginning of a completely new phase of her life where there is more time and space for her, and support her finding work she enjoys. Joining a support group of other women transiting the midlife crisis can be most helpful as she realises these changes are normal and they provide a door for new beginnings.

Conclusion

This is a deeply spiritual period, a period in which the connection to our human spirit, or light, demands to be reinvigorated. We must connect to that which is highest within us and uplift our life, work and relationships to these realms of light which reflect the highest, noblest and the best of the human spirit. Only then can we counter the forces of gravity, that pull our physical body back to earth, that draw the emotional life into a heavy, dark, sombre if not sometimes lonely place in the later years of life. The battle for the human spirit within each one of us in the 42-49 year period is well worth fighting on behalf of our spirit, for the outcome sets the flow of the older years of the lifespan. The quality of these years physically, mentally and emotionally rests on the course we choose at this phase of the life span. This is the phase in which we must strengthen our connection to our spirit so that we do not succumb to the heaviness of gravity and ageing. It is our free choice and we must marshal our inner strength to choose that which is in our highest interests for the remainder of the lifespan.

We must change and change our thinking, feeling and willing radically, if we are not to return to a second adolescence and do an inappropriate regression to avoid the challenges of this phase of the life span. Muhammad Ali captures the picture of change that is required:

> The man who views the world at 50 the same as he did at 20 has wasted 30 years of his life (cited in Peterson, 2010, p.456).

SUMMARY

- I am experiencing the dark night of my soul and at times I will feel moody, fearful and inadequate.

- I am vulnerable because my known plan is failing and I am uncertain of how to develop a new plan.

- I can no longer rely on my sexuality to pull me through relationships and give me a boost in confidence.

- My spirit is calling me to be more of who I am but I am fearful I lack the skills and the courage to step forward.

- I may become physically or emotionally ill from the turbulence of this period as I have to face my limitations, my failures and my lost dreams and aspirations.

- I may want to flee back to adolescence so I can start out all over again on the path of life but I know this is a futile distraction.

- I am struggling to reinvigorate my life, my career and my relationships with the light of my highest consciousness so I can create a pathway of joy, fulfilment and satisfaction into my old age.

- I often feel inadequate for the task and will sometimes blame others and project my fear on them as anger, blame and criticism.

REFERENCES

Bryant, W (1993) *The Veiled Pulse of Time: Life Cycles and Destiny,* NY, Lindisfarne.

Lievegoed, B (2003) *Phases: The Spiritual Rhythms in Adult Life,* London, Sophia Books

O'Neil, G& O'Neil, G (1998) *The Human Life,*NY, Mercury Press.

O'Connor, P (1981) *Understanding the Midlife Crisis* (Sydney, Macmillan, 1981) pp. 26-28

Peterson, C (2010) *Looking Forward through the Lifespan: Developmental Psychology,*Sydney, Pearson.

Vickers-Willis,Robyn (2004) *Navigating the Midlife Crisis: Women Becoming Themselves,* Sydney, Allen &Unwin.

Sheehy, G (1976) *Passages – Predictable Crises of Adult Life,*New York, Bantam Books.

Staley, B (1997) *Tapestries: Weaving Life's Journey,* Stroud, Hawthorn Press.

"Aging is not lost youth but a new stage of opportunity and strength."
—Betty Friedan

CHAPTER 9

Mature adulthood: 49-56 years
"Confronting your dark side"

Introduction

The disturbing but very individualising Mars energy of the 40s gives way to the expansive Jupiter energy of the first half of the 50s. This energy grounds our individual destinies and work so that we start to have roots grounded in the wisdom that we as an individual can and have shared in this life. It is a period for the cultivation of not just experience but of reflective insightful experience that is wisdom (O'Neil and O'Neil, 1998). This gives us the perfect vantage point for looking back over our lives and gaining deeper perspective on our experiences. We also seek to understand more fully our family roots. Often we return for a visit to a country from which our parents migrated. We might become interested in the family genealogy or with linking up with long lost relatives. We start to listen to and see our parents' life story in a different way. It is also a phase in which we start to focus on peace and forgiveness when reviewing the past and let go of strong emotions that we may have held towards others that were not skilful. If we hang onto grudges at this stage of the lifespan they will make us bitter or ill. It is the time to move past pettiness and stop clinging to old hurts. Staley (1997,p. 212) summarises it well:

> The big question during this period is whether we will have enough flexibility to learn from the past, or become too rigid and replay past errors.

This is a period of understanding, a period to stand in our own space as free human beings and to accept ourselves warts and all. We can develop more compassion and fewer judgments towards others as our self-acceptance of our strengths and weaknesses grows in this period. However, we cannot avoid looking at our shadow or dark side because it will not disappear. To repress it will lead to ill health, rigidity and unproductive relationships. We must face the fullness of who we are. It is the period of acceptance of self, life, others and the world, of being firmly grounded in what is and accepting one's life with gratitude. Under the influence of Jupiter, the energies work to produce harmony, symmetry and well thought out balance in one's life and human relationships (Lievegoed, 1987). It is what Stacey describes as "finding beauty in the art of living" (1997, p.221). This period re-echoes the 7-14year old development period, and is anchored again in the experience of the beauty and joy of life. Between seven and 14 years, this experience is spontaneous and part of our youthful innocence.

At this age, our celebration of joy and beauty of life is hammered on the anvil of the soul's purification through the furnace of life. We have distilled the gold from our experience and we can shape our self into the form of wisdom that reflects effort. It is the phase when our self-development throughout the life span becomes obvious(O'Neil and O'Neil, 1998). It is manifest in the wisdom of experience that radiates from the work of someone who has mastered themselves and their craft. They carry it in their presence, in their gestures and in their countenance. They have the look of someone who embodies the best of their profession. They can inspire younger people to improve their skills, and they prove ideal mentors during this age phase as well as having the presence to transform communities. These are the best times for leadership. At this age phase these persons have earned their accolades at the anvil of their inner soul work, which moulds their profession or craft into a work of beauty and inspiration. O'Neil and O'Neil (1998, p.13) describes this powerfully:

> It is at this age that judgment and authority can manifest most effectively in the community and in institutions. These forces of the personality are of such substance that they awaken trust and confidence resulting in natural leadership. Characteristic of this age is an infectious vitality that can animate others,...sufficiently purified of the personal element as not to offend.

Physical development

During this phase all women complete the transition through menopause. The majority of women experience greater emotional wellbeing and a greater sense of freedom as they pass through menopause. The male menopause is less likely to be viewed positively by men. Martha Lear (1974) describes the experience well:

> The hormone production levels are dropping, the head is balding, the sexual vigor is diminishing, the stress is unending, the children are leaving, the parents are dying, the job horizons are narrowing, the friends are having their first heart attacks; the past

floats by in a fog of hopes not realized, opportunities not grasped, women not bedded, potentials not fulfilled and the future is a confrontation with one's own mortality (Peterson, 2010,p.468).

The lowering of testosterone levels after the age of 40 can profoundly affect sexual performance. It takes longer for a middle-aged man to become sexually aroused. Fertility declines, erections are less common, less seminal fluid is ejected and men come to desire sexual intercourse less frequently as they grow older. Overall though, neither female menopause nor the male hormonal changes during middle age prevent mature sexual enjoyment. The primary constraints are a person's attitude to sexuality and the availability of a supportive partner (Peterson, 2010).

Three major processes of change are continuing to occur during this phase of the life span: The brain continues to develop throughout late adulthood through synaptic pruning, myelination and other neuro-cognitive changes. While the plasticity of the brain declines, some recovery from damage is still possible in later years. Mental exercises maintain cognitive flexibility and raise the level of functioning throughout adulthood.

The senses of hearing and vision decline rapidly in the 40 and 50 year age brackets and the population will need devices that assist – whether glasses, hearing aids or Cochlear implants. Taste and smell also decline, particularly in men, during these latter years (Peterson, 2010).

Psychological: Cognitive development

In this period, adults become more efficient in solving real world problems involving compromise, responsibility and dialectical conflict. There is also the time to develop a more complex system of ethics and understanding of the difficulties of making ethical decisions. This age group should start to see the world of moral dilemmas as complex and become more tolerant of difference.

The 55.8 moon node often follows a period of physical and cognitve exhaustion from burnout at work or with family commitments. We have been actively hard at work in the world and at this point exhaustion and depletion become evident. This period often comes to a crisis with health problems or may follow an illness that demands signficiant attention. There is considerable energy to embark on a change of lifestyle, a winding down of career, a more active awareness of the quality of our lives rather than the quantity of our lives. Out of this struggle comes a new awareness of the importance of the greater good and of directing our energies towards the benefit of the whole, rather than just our personal goals. This is the growing point of this crisis that marks the transition from focus on personal goals to the wider society and world (Stacey, 1997).

Psychological social: Emotional development

For the person who has worked their way through the crisis of the 40s to find a new synthesis of life and work that represents their individuality, then this is a period of expansion and creativity. Often promotion to senior positions represents the outcome of these transitions. The bitter, critical complaining bosses in their 50s have failed to make the midlife transition in productive ways, while the bosses in their 50s who provide wise leadership, understanding and compassion have made this transition and are able to embrace others with the goodness and understanding that comes from the midlife crisis when navigated well.

For most couples, the empty-nest syndrome is in full swing by this time with children – now young adults – leaving home to study, travel or work elsewhere. This helicopter generation of young people will occasionally return home throughout the twenties to save for their next adventure or between adventures or travel. Essentially though the couple are now thrown back together. If the marriage survives this transition back to couple-hood, there is often an increase in couple satisfaction and a more relaxed togetherness. For some parents, grandparent-hood will also arrive during this phase.

The empty-nest syndrome lays the path for new ways of relating to one's now adult children, and new ways of relating and reconnecting as a couple as well as providing new opportunities for travel, entertainment and relaxation that were not available when one was tied to school timetables. One mother suggested there should be a "moolies" celebration to accompany the "schoolies" celebration by Year 12 students leaving school and moving on to employment or further study. "Moolies" she defined as mothers who were free to organise their lives without being bound by the constraints of the school timetable, sporting commitments and other events that required them to transport their children back and forth.

"Grand-parenting" is the major new psycho-social experience for many people in this age group. Women in particular report high levels of satisfaction in watching their grandchildren grow up, in babysitting them, spoiling them and experiencing pride in the achievements of their grandchildren. The level of spoiling and indulging grandchildren depends on the level of responsibility the grandparent has for the grandchild. The less responsibility the grandparent has for the child, the higher the level of indulgence.

Spiritual development

Our crisis and challenges of the 40s, if successfully navigated, lead us to a more integrated self, so that we can bring forth in this phase new strength, courage and stability within ourselves. It is during this phase that all the excesses of our past come home to roost and only renewal of our human spirit can sail our ship through these times. Whenever we ignore or repress emotions and experiences, we are setting ourselves up for physical or mental illness as we no longer have the reserves or buffers that characterise the younger phases of the life span.

We must deal with our shadow. In the 40s, we deal primarily with what Firma and Gilla (1997:111) describe as the positive shadow, or Sherwood (2008) describes as the light shadow. This comprises the repressed parts of ourselves that are not innately harmful but which we have personally and socially devalued and repressed in our lives. Examples include repressing feeling as opposed to allowing thinking to dominate, repressing creativity as opposed to allowing conformity to dominate, or repressing spirituality as opposed to allowing materialism to rule.

In the 50s, we face the dark shadow, the parts of ourselves that are personally and socially harmful such as greed, cruelty, injustice, hatred, revenge, jealousy and pride. They are constantly trying to find a way into our conscious mind through dreams, jokes, slips of the tongue, reactions and projections onto others of these dark qualities. Sherwood (2012) notes that the dark shadow is the program that runs our self-righteousness, our self-saboteur and our self-judgements. It is what Robert Bly (1988, p.17) calls "the long bag we drag behind us". It weighs us down, makes us ill, dampens the *joie de vivre* and sours our relationships. It leaves us hard, brittle and cold, lonely and bitter as we age companioned by resentment, blame and loneliness. It is essential in this phase of the life span that we stop pretending we are only nice and kind and that all our ills are caused by external events. Instead, we must dig deeply into the garden of our soul and find the plants of hatred, revenge, jealousy, greed, injustice, pride, cruelty and heal the multitudes of fears that feed them in this toxic soil. We must rescue them from this darkness, bring these parts of ourselves to the light, speak with them, heal their fears, retain their strengths and re-dedicate our knowing of them to the creation of compassion. This is the compassion that is a profound, non-judgmental approach to others. This is the compassion that can embrace the diversity of humanity and find ways to place "and" rather than "or" in the decisions that confront us in our world. We can start to build a world where compassion and mercy reign. Only then can we enter what Jung terms the House of the Gathering:

> Such a man knows that whatever is wrong in the world is in himself, and if he only learns to deal with his own shadow he has done something real for the world. He has succeeded in shouldering at least an infinitesimal part of the gigantic, unsolved social problems of our day (1938:140).

We admire the people who have succeeded in this challenging developmental task for they have become world leaders for peace and stability. Gandhi, Martin Luther King, Nelson Mandela and Aung San Suu Kyi have made profound leadership contributions to stability and conflict resolution in their nations. This is the leadership that this phase of the life span calls us to work towards– in our families, our communities and our countries. This leadership is based on wisdom that requires us to confront and integrate our dark shadow qualities. This is not a task for the faint-hearted but it is the surest pathway to the creation of inner wisdom that will determine not only our contribution to life in this phase, but in all the ensuing phases.

Developmental decisions

I am 52 years old and I feel jaded and run down... I'm just not wanting to go to work anymore... I am not happy in my relationship and I feel that life is passing me by, and if something does not change now I will always be stuck here. What do I do about it?

At the 52-year period, there is a strong surge of psycho-spiritual energy to push us out of stuck patterns and behaviours, especially unresolved issues from the 40s. It is like a wave beating on the shores of our "stuckness" and demanding us to take our surfboards and find new water. It will not be quieted and can create considerable disquiet in life if it is not acknowledged and life reviewed. It is demanding that the dead energy in our life, the dead relationships, devitalised work be pruned away so that new growth can sprout for the future of our life span that is healthy, alive and vibrant. This energy for change provides a strong undercurrent to our daily existence. It has the power to sap our physical energy if we do not act. Things that were just tolerable in the 40s and that have lost their living place in our lives, whether work or relationships, will no longer be tolerated. To repress this urge is to court physical or mental health breakdown by the age of 56.

Conclusion

This phase of the lifespan has been described as the youth of old age. It is a phase when every minute must count because there is no time to be wasted completing tasks and remaining in relationships that are lifeless or meaningless. It is the critical time to make the moves that will ensure we enter our older years with enthusiasm, vitality and youthfulness of spirit because we have created the opportunities in our lives that give us joy, fulfilment and satisfaction. Jim Carrey concisely nails the process in his comments below:

Fifty years; here is a time when you have to separate yourself from what other people expect of you, and do what you love. Because if you find yourself 50 years old and you are not doing what you love, then what's the point?

(http://www.sayingsplus.com/50th-birthday-sayings.html)

SUMMARY

- I must face all that I am, both my goodness and my darkness.

- I must own all that I am and transform it into an integrated whole.

- I am capable of transcending pettiness and smallness and of finding the important qualities in life.

- I can provide leadership that is strong, skilled and which reflects the wisdom that I have acquired in the shaping of my experiences.

- I can choose to harvest my life experiences, both good and bad, positive and negative, and grind a flour that is either nourishing for myself and others or that is bitter in taste for everyone.

- I can contribute to the greater good of the community through my works and skills that I have shaped by the wisdom of my experience.

- I enjoy grand-parenting as it contributes greatly to my psycho-emotional wellbeing and the sense of continuity I feel with my children and their lives and my own life.

REFERENCES

Bly, R (1988) *A Little Book on the Human Shadow,* San Francisco, Harper.

Bryant, W (1993) *The Veiled Pulse of Time: Life Cycles and Destiny,* NY, Lindisfarne.

Jung (1938) "Psychology and Religion",*Collected Works 11:Psychology and Religion: West and East.*

Lievegoed, B (1985) *Man on the Threshold,*Stroud, Hawthorn Press.

Peterson, C (2010) *Looking Forward through the Lifespan: Developmental Psychology.* Sydney, Pearson.

Sherwood, P (2008) *Holistic Counselling: A New Vision for Mental Health,*Bunbury, Sophia Publications.

Sherwood, P (2012) *Holistic Counselling: Through the Shadow to Compassion* Bunbury, Sophia Publications.

Staley, B (1997) *Tapestries: Weaving Life's Journey,* Stroud, Hawthorn Press.

"There is a fountain of youth; it is your mind, your talents, the creativity you bring to your life and the lives of people you love. When you learn to tap this source, you will truly have defeated age."

—Sophia Loren

CHAPTER 10

Senior adulthood: 56-63 years
"Choosing the gems"

Introduction

Just as we reach the pinnacle of the hill of our new plans and new vision for ourselves at 56 years, we are enveloped by the energy of Saturn. Saturn demands we move from a focus on our external vision to a focus on our internal vision. Saturn's contracting energy makes us regularly ask: "What can I do less of? What are the essential components of my life that nurture my inner spirit? What can I stop doing and feel happier?" Saturn contracts the horizon so that we must confront this developmental stage that makes the transition into being a "senior". This is the phase in which our understandings are matured to a new level of ripeness. We emerge from the previous phase of the life span knowing what we want and understanding what we are worth, and in this phase we confront our inner knowledge. We are forced to explore the inner world as the outer constricts us. The pressing task is to develop a distinction between what we know and what is wisdom within us. We should shed the scales of self-righteousness to expose our natural humility and goodness, sloth the skin of envy and resentment in exchange for contentment and inner peace. Our deepest inner goodness can now shine forth uncluttered by the noise of life.

If this transition is not made then one is clinging to a life that is fast slipping through one's fingers, and feelings of frustration, bitterness or even despair will rise to haunt the latter years that would otherwise be characterised by peace and contentment. Alternatively, one may try to avoid these tasks by spending endless hours in trivial pursuits of the younger phases of the life span. Jung, (1979,p.75) describes this transition with great insight.

> It seems to me that the basic facts of the psyche undergo a very marked alteration in the course of life, so much so that we could almost speak of a psychology of life's

morning and a psychology of its afternoon. As a rule, the life of a young person is characterised by a general expansion and a striving towards concrete ends; and his neurosis seems mainly to rest on his hesitation or shrinking back from this necessity. But the life of an older person is characterised by a contraction of forces, by the affirmation of what has been achieved and by the curtailment of further growth. His neurosis comes mainly from his clinging to a youthful attitude which is now out of season…

At 58 years we experience our second Saturn return, the first was at 29 years. During these periods the new beginnings for the next 29 years are laid. This includes the planting of patterns that will affect our health, our family life, our intimate relationships and our expression of our spirits through our careers in the world. We can expect significant change of direction in our life plan at 58 years that will alter the plans for our future (O'Neil and O'Neil, p.1998). The period between 56 to 63 years is critical to ensure we enlarge the gems of our experience, the beautiful and courageous moments of our life. We enhance the opportunities in our life for fulfilment, connectedness and intimacy with self, others and the world. It is not a time for quantity that too often results in superficiality and disconnection. This is the time for quality choices in everything we do. It is during this phase that we need to choose the things we love, that are precious to us to take with us into our older years. We need to open our heart and mind to new ideas and new possibilities and let go of the attachment to material security and finances as the only "fulfilling" pathway into old age. This is difficult with the media hype and superannuation advertising pushing astronomical sums of money as the basic line for retirement into a secure old age.

Physical development

All our cumulative thoughts words and deeds of our preceding life are stamped indelibly on the physical organism by 63 years of age. At 63, there is often a physical health crisis that reflects the unresolved emotional, cognitive and physical traumas of our lives. There is a marked change in one's natural vitality– energy levels– and the desire to work less physically is often the response as people start to review their abilities to continue their current lifestyle into old age. It is a time when the senses start to show their age in unavoidable ways. The eyesight dims and a person starts to wear glasses or to increase the strength of their glasses. Sense of taste and smell may decline as well as hearing. These senses decline more in men than women and the changes depend on lifestyle, diet and nutrition, and exercise (Peterson, 2010, p.479).

Psychological: Cognitive development

During this period of the life span our thinking becomes deeply aware of the processes that underlie life and its problems. There is awareness of the ebb and flow of problems, an increasing awareness that everything is impermanent, it is in constant change or flux. There is a releasing of the views that problems can be solved by experts, instantly or simplistically. There is a deep inner knowing that the process is often more important than the solution (Bryant 1993). This cognitive approach to the world strengthens and we become more located in the present moment, letting go of many of the superfluities and sensory distractions of the world. It is the time to prune the tree of your life and to cut out the dead wood, the boring lifeless repetitive parts of your life that are on automatic pilot and that do not give you vitality. It is the time to fertilise the roots of the tree with the things that give you vitality and energy. Then, it can bear beautiful flowers and precious fruits that taste delicious and that nurture your mind and heart. There are many things that need to be let go and to be sent to recycling, and a few things we need to graft onto our tree. This is the time for serious stocktaking so we travel into the older years without being weighed down by useless baggage that only hastens our declining physical energy. Campbell (Fuller, 2011, p.139) expresses the need to focus on our consciousness and its depth and capacity for growth, rather than on the declining physical abilities when he suggests we reflect upon: "Am I the bulb that carries the light or am I the light of which the bulb is a vehicle?"

Psychological social: Emotional development

The immediate and core psycho-social development during this phase is retirement, and the key question is usually when do I retire or do I work part-time? At 59 years of age more than 15 per cent of Australians have retired, and by 64 years of age 35 per cent have retired. By 69 years the figure has reached nearly 70 per cent and by 70 years 90 per cent. (Peterson, 2010, p.473). Retirement makes the major transition into the latter years of the life span, and planning for retirement moves the focus of the life from externally controlled activities and experiences to those that are self-governed. Myths governing retirement are popular and include the following:

1. Retirement is a health hazard and you are likely to die quickly after retirement.
2. Retirement always necessitates financial difficulties that were not there prior to retirement.
3. Women adjust better to retirement than men.

There are phases in the retirement process which include both highs and lows in experience and which have been well documented (Peterson, 2010, p.474). They are summarised diagrammatically below:

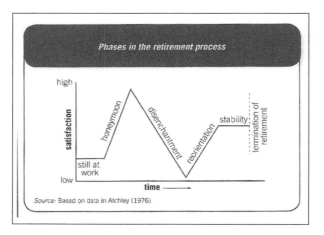

Good physical health, adequate finances and a strong, long-term marital relationship have been found to be good indicators of ease of transition through the phases of retirement. Of course voluntary retirement usually results in a quicker transition than involuntary retirement.

Spiritual development

At 63 years, the mark of our spiritual development is strongly writ on our countenance. A very good example is Alfred Nobel, who became extraordinarily wealthy inventing and selling dynamite and other explosives manufactured in his many factories around the world. He witnessed his products being turned into weapons of war that further fuelled international war. At 56 years, his death was misreported in the newspapers when it related to his brother. It was the stimulus for a significant change in his life. In the period between 56 and 63 years, he became very reclusive, meditating on the purpose of his life and his contribution to the world. It was during this period that he developed the concept of the Nobel Prize. It included the Nobel Peace Prize for the person who had made the greatest contribution to world peace each year. The Nobel Prize process was inaugurated by Alfred Nobel to reward and encourage those persons in the fields of literature, chemistry, politics, medicine and physics who made the greatest contributions each year to humanity's wellbeing. It was a fitting deed in this phase of the life span where he harvested his knowledge, earthly experiences and resources to make a profound contribution to humanity.

The self, formed from the synthesis of our experiences, our attitudes to life and our deeds in the world becomes transparent at the culmination of this cycle, and for the remainder of the life span we reap the harvest of the seeds we have sown. Bryant (1993,p.71) describes this powerfully:

> All our experience, the reactions and conflicts which come to us by way of the external world, sinks into this interior cauldron of synthesis. It is there that experience is distilled and assimilated into the self. Cycle after cycle, our thoughts, feelings and actions are the seeds planted in the inner continuum of the psyche, and in our sixties we begin to reap the harvest.

Essentially, our earthly experiences are harvested at this time, for the cultivation of our inner wisdom and for the distribution of our wisdom among younger generations. The mysteries of life move from without to within and the focus of the mind and spirit also moves from external to internal. (Lievegoed, 1985).

During this phase another significant change occurs in the maturing human spirit. Our enthusiasm for life arises through conscious effort; it is not spontaneous as in the earlier phases of the life span. We may still have ideals but our engagement in them is much more considered, as we no longer have energy to waste as in earlier phases. This can be described as "achieved or mature idealism" which at its heart embraces deep empathy and compassion for others. This sense of greater connectedness with humanity is the driver for healthy psychosocial maturity in our later years. Otherwise, we can be left with bitterness, despair and a sense of spiritual disconnectedness (Staley, 1993).

Developmental decisions

How can one best prepare psychologically for retirement?

It is important that one prepare for retirement so that one transits healthily. This is particularly a problem for males. The transition toward retirement should be marked by strengthening relationships with family and good friends, being socially active, developing new interests or expanding on previous interests and creative ideas that have slipped by the wayside. Shedding things/stuff/objects/material possessions we have garnered through our lives is excellent preparation as it relieves us of the dead energy of clutter, insuring, transporting, cleaning and containing it. There is a growing need to simplify the lifestyle so that energy is no longer expended in maintaining property that is not directly used. There is also a need to reach out and engage in new activities and interests that one has always wanted to do but has never had the time to pursue. It is an ideal time to engage in volunteer work so that the person continues to experience a sense of value and connectedness to the community.

What are the key signs of successful ageing?

Jung answers this question very well:

- The link between meaningful engagement in one's family, community and society and the healthy ageing brain;
- The importance of resilience in the ability to cope with the limitations and losses that accompany ageing;
- The ability to assimilate and accept life's failures as well as successes in order to achieve a greater degree of wholeness;
- The need to revisit and rework the traumas experienced in life in order to make peace with them and unlock creativity;
- The need to replace the traditional medical model of ageing as a descent into poor health and social withdrawal with a more holistic view of ageing as a time of continuing growth, exploration, creative expression and engagement;
- The link between engagement in the arts and other creative endeavours and improved physical and mental health outcomes;
- The importance of play and fun in maintaining good mental and physical health as we age;
- The use of dream work, self-reflection, writing, the arts and other techniques to promote conscious living and achieve psycho-spiritual growth;
- The need to incorporate patient spirituality into the delivery of healthcare services and;
- The possibility of encountering the sacred in dreams, visions, creativity and other experiences(Carbine and Sawin,2012,p.6).

Conclusion

This is a splendid opportunity to develop and enlarge activities that are the foundation of the joy of our experience. It is the time to focus on the aspects of life and our experience that are most fulfilling and nourishing. It is the time to shed unnecessary baggage, to release ourselves for commitments and responsibilities that we have now outgrown as our children make their own way as adults in the world. It is the time to celebrate all that we most love and to take care of our physical life energies so they are not spent on that which does not put a smile on our faces, joy in our movement and love in our hearts.

SUMMARY

- I harvest the fruits of my experiences in the world.
- I spend increasing amounts of time simplifying my life of excess possessions and material objects.
- I slow down my physical engagement in the world and replace it with inner reflections and activities that feed my soul.
- My idealism for change in the world is now less driven by external actions and more driven by internal structures.
- Rather than solutions to life's problems, I see life as a process whereby everything is in change.
- I search for greater connectedness with the world through the development of more compassion and empathy for others.
- I am more content to live in the present moment and appreciate each moment.
- I focus on the positives of my life journey so I can expand these qualities within myself and my community.
- I must work to generate enthusiasm for life otherwise I end up with little motivation.
- I reflect in my physical body and countenance all of my experiences through my life span. The body will no longer provide a hiding place for my heart or mind.
- I expand my consciousness to embrace meaningful and living experiences and avoid ruts, old patterns and activities that exclude my heart.

REFERENCES

Bryant, W (1993) *The Veiled Pulse of Time: Life Cycles and Destiny,* NY, Lindisfarne.

Carbine and Leslie Sawin (2012) *Jung and Aging: Bringing to Life the Possibilities and Potentials for Vibrant Aging,*Proceedings of the March 28, 2012 Symposium at the Library of Congress Washington, D.C.

Fuller, A (2011) *Life: A Guide. What to expect in each seven year stage,* Sydney, Finch.

Jung, C (1929) *Collected works 16, p.75.*

Lievegoed, B (1985) *Man on the Threshold,*Stroud, Hawthorn Press.

Peterson, C (2010) *Looking Forward through the Lifespan: Developmental Psychology,*Sydney, Pearson.

Sherwood, P (2012) *Holistic Counselling: Through the Shadow to Compassion,* Bunbury, Sophia Publications.

Staley, B (1997) *Tapestries: Weaving Life's Journey,* Stroud, Hawthorn Press.

"Beautiful young people are accidents of nature, but beautiful old people are works of art."
—Eleanor Roosevelt

CHAPTER 11

Old age: 63-70 years
"Sharing the wisdom"

Introduction

At 63 years of age, we enter the retirement period of our life, potentially the time of life with the most freedom from responsibilities and with our life within our own control. It is the phase in which the primary tasks of our life have been completed and one is free to reap the harvest of one's deeds and to gather sheaths of the grain ripened into the wisdom of a life well lived, whatever its challenges, turmoils and angst. It is the phase when we start to become reapers of our life's experience, and in our most productive times we become transmitters to the next generation of the fruits of our love and wisdom. We become the keepers of life's knowledge that we can share with generosity and experience to encourage those younger than ourselves on their journey through life. Jane Fonda(2012) aptly coined the term "prime time" to describe the unique potential and the extraordinary expansiveness in time of this phase of the life span in which she included love, sex, spirit, fitness and friendship. This period of life is a period of adventure, a mirroring of the 21-28 phase of life where there is energy to discover the world, but on this round it is the world of retirement (O'Neil and O'Neil). It also recapitulates the 42 to 49 period of connecting to the world in a new way that is unique and individualised for our particular talents and interests, but on this occasion it is not about career but rather about one's personal interests and activities.

One is standing on the threshold of a new beginning, a rebirth of the spirit into a realm of experience that is more contracted in the outer world but more inclusive in the emotional and inner world. We have more space and time for those we love, more openness to tender moments that make us such good grandparents. Our own children recognise this change in our heart space and may complain when they see us with their children that "You were never so easy going, never so much fun and you never allowed me to eat icecream before meals, to play in the guest room, and to make messy games that you allow your grandchildren." In this phase, we shed the constraints of rules, mountains of work and family stresses to create gentle times of love and connectedness with those we love. Friends become closer to our heart too, as we recognise that intimacy directs the quality of our life experiences.

Physical development

While spiritually and emotionally the horizon is expansive, physically we are facing a gradual sunset– beautiful, colourful but in decline. This is reflected in changes to the physical body that are progressive and inevitable. Older people experience a decline in muscular strength, reaction time, stamina, hearing, distance perception and the sense of smell. They also are more susceptible to diseases such as cancer and pneumonia due to a weakened immune system (Blanchard-Fields, Cavanaugh, Fredda,2009). However, medical advances mean that this stage of the life cycle can still be lived by the majority of us with health and vitality. Denial of our physical ageing is unhelpful since it traps us in missing out on the joys of the present moment because of our pre-occupation with looking younger and impressing others as younger. As Jung (1971) notes, "the wine of youth does not always clear with advancing years; sometimes it grows turbid". This is particularly so when ageing adults cling to an adolescent lifestyle. Those of us who focus on the physical body at this point in time will ultimately be unsatisfied, discontent, because it is the inner emotional life that must be focused on and nurtured in order to create real fulfilment. Facelifts, Botox and plastic surgery will not facilitate lasting contentment in this phase of life.

Perhaps nowhere is this decline so evident as in the gradual disintegration of the senses. As we age, the sense organs weaken so we are forced to replace outer sensory experiences with inner sensory experiences. We may no longer be able to leap up the stairs in a single bound but as we rest or walk slowly up the stairs, we are able to enjoy the beauty of the light coming through the window. We may not see outwardly so acutely but inwardly we have many treasured memories to review and many creative ideas to visualise. Staley (1997) beautifully captures this transformation of the senses from the outer to the inner. She works through the 12 senses identified in the anthroposophical model of a human being and documented brilliantly by Soesman (2009). The sense of touch becomes a feeling of reverence for what is around us, the sense of life leads us to doing more for other people and a sense of movement causes us to nurture ourselves rather than expend our energy on wasted movements. Our sense of balance leads to a feeling of inner balance or calm so we are centred within and no longer chase material items to clutter our world. Our sense of smell can be transformed from the world entering us, into the opportunity for us to enter the world through our compassion and understanding. Our sense of taste is transformed into a humility and interest in the diversity of other people if we seek understanding and our sense of sight can be transformed into inner sight, wisdom and gratitude as we look back on our life experiences. Our sense of warmth diminishes externally but our cultivation of a warm heart has the space and time to flourish. While our sense of hearing diminishes we can increase our openness of mind and our receptivity to be present to that which comes to us from the world. The sense of thought is enhanced by going within and increasing the depth of our thinking, penetrating ideas from within and reawakening our sense of awe. Finally, the sense of ego that relates to appreciating other persons' characters can grow if we reach out to newcomers in our world with kindness. Thus, as older people we can be a blessing in younger peoples lives encouraging them through life's challenges and opportunities.

Psychological: Cognitive development

Mentally, our attitude to ageing has a profound effect on the quality of our later years. We will either approach these retirement years with enthusiasm and maximise the opportunities that come our way, or we will retreat from new challenges and become increasingly isolated, grumpy/bored. Mentally, we will stagnate and regress into more infantile stages of development. Attitude is everything which Fonda elaborates in *Prime Time* (2012, p. 139) citing Dr Perlmutter:

> Positivity may be due to the accumulation of perspective. The first time that something happens like financial loss, for instance, it is horrible. But after you have seen cycles of something like that happening, you have some perspective that this doesn't mean the end of life. It just means a new challenge that we will get through.

In essence, as one ages one is more likely not to be attached to problems as the focus of life but to take the attitude that "this too shall pass" and to move more easily with the flow of life. The new is built on the foundation of insight and acceptance that all things are impermanent.

At this stage of retirement one is able to form a new repertoire of routines and activities, renew interest in learning. The University of the Third Age (u3auwa.org/region) provides splendid opportunities for retired adults to pursue educational activities, and the many community centres offer creative painting, woodwork and other craft activities for groups of retired adults. During this phase, thinkers, philosophers and writers often take a new turn in their work adding new ideas that are closer to the world of the spirit. It was at 68, for example, that Gregory Bateson (1972) wrote *Steps to a New Ecology of Mind* that became a foundational text for the new models of holistic thinking in relation to the environment, anthropology, psychiatry, social change and counselling. It countered the dominant materialistic atomistic worldview and proposed a holistic interrelated worldview.

This is the phase when one can access all the planetary influences that have been gathered up through life's journey. O'Neil and O'Neil (1990, p.228) articulate this brilliantly:

> From the Moon come the tides for a new lifestyle, while Saturn enhances reverence for life and moral stature, from Mercury healing forces instil new vitality and longevity, while Jupiter grants renewed creativity and a kingly bearing; from Venus are bestowed the purified beauty, the glow of old age, while Mars arms the octogenarian with extraordinary stamina and boldness.

This is the profile of the best of what we can achieve in these later years and reminds us that entering the retirement years from 63 onwards need not be a decline in our cognitive and creative abilities but rather an expansiveness of our abilities to think and create with more depth, courage, innovation and clarity.

The retiree who avoids exploring more deeply new ideas and creating new interests in the world can easily degenerate into a second childhood, happily playing golf or bingo, aimlessly travelling and "gourmandizing" their way around the planet. At this point, the retiree is clinging to the past, to what he knows, and is fearful of taking steps forward in his or her mental and inward growth. In this approach to retirement and old age, the person is incarnating the negative influences of the planets. O'Neil and O'Neil (1990, p.229) describe this succinctly:

> The moonlike superficiality, the mercurial avarice and the constant preoccupation with health, and then the Venus inspired over-preoccupation with appearances... the saturnine temper and pessimism, the magisterial hardening into fixed ideas or perpetual criticism, the marital belligerence of late age.

This is a backward path whereby the retiree is heading to the past, when all the growth and life and energy is in the present.

Psychological social: Emotional development

As we enter this phase, we experience daily that the values, drivers and motivators of our early active life will no longer suffice to navigate our way through old age. We must seek a new set of values that are socially and personally fulfilling within the constraints of our declining physical ability to engage in worldly activities. The direction we need to seek is within, to cultivate the parts of our self that are fulfilling and that have been ignored, repressed or overridden during the active years of career achievement and goals. In this phase, you can be what Fuller describes as a "character", your own character, as zany, bright and beautiful and idiosyncratic as you choose to be. You are at last free from others' expectations, and the roles of parent and worker prescribed by society. Real emotional health is achieved by giving new things a go and daring to do the things you have dreamed about doing and by being active, so your physical body can support your adventures.

Spiritual development

However, during this phase we must not forget that old age is leading us to focus on the non-material, the spiritual, so that in our later years when those we know and party with have disappeared or are no longer able to do so, we are our own best companion. We must become familiar with our spirit, with the depths of our experience and with a salutary review of our lives.

Jung (1971:17) describes this task brilliantly:

> Ageing people should know that their lives are not mounting and expanding, but that an inexorable inner process enforces the contraction of life. For a young person it is almost a sin, or at least a danger, to be too preoccupied with himself; but for the ageing person it is a duty and a necessity to devote serious attention to himself. After having lavished its light upon the world, the sun withdraws its rays in order to illumine itself. Instead of doing likewise, many old people prefer to be hypochondriacs, niggards, pedants, applauders of the past or else eternal adolescents– all lamentable substitutes for the illumination of the self.

We must face the inner journey with determination and not skate over it as though by engaging in continuous travel, cruises, coffee shops and eateries we can ignore it. If we try to do this, the future phases of our old age will breed frustration, discontent, pre-occupation with physical health, especially as the body weakens and we are forced to be stationary.

Developmental decisions

How much money do I need to retire happily?

At the psycho-emotional level of retirement, the progressive and healthy development is away from material needs and towards being needed. It is important for the retiree to seek opportunities to develop themselves through giving to others while simultaneously downsizing. The children are grown and flown the nest and the smaller the nest, the more it will support the psycho-emotional growth of a healthy retiree. As one moves through this phase it is most helpful to discard or pass on possessions that are no longer required to the younger generation. Freedom arises by being free of burdens of possessions to care for while having time and space just to enjoy being in the present moment.

Is it ok not to retire now and keep working until 70?

If one's physical health is good and one loves every moment of one's work, then it is fine to continue to work, albeit decreasing the number of days and hours as one approaches 70. The core lesson at this period in the lifespan is that no work should be undertaken that does not bring intense joy and contentment because there are no spare life forces to squander and engaging in a deadening occupation will have deadening consequences for the physical body.

Conclusion

This is the phase of beginning retirement, of seeking to let go of one's lifelong pattern of work and to downsize material possessions as one moves towards understanding more deeply the inner life, to sharing these understandings through friends, travel and new creative ventures. All these actions can stimulate the birth of this second period of exploring the world but while the energy in the first period from 21 to 28 focuses on exploring the outer world, this period makes the focus on exploring the inner world. This embraces that which lies within us and which can be born through our hobbies, our reflections and volunteering in our communities.

SUMMARY

- I remember that now is the time for me to be the character I am and not be concerned about other people's opinions.
- Now is the time to challenge myself to try new things and develop stronger intimate relationship with my friends and family.
- I really need to spend time with myself and delve into my deepest aspirations.

- I need to keep learning the things that interest me and to continue to open my mind to new ideas.

- I need to keep physically active and eat well because my health is very dependent on the care I invest in it.

- I need to downsize my physical environment and upsize my inner life and environment.

REFERENCES

Bateson, G (1972) *Steps to an Ecology of Mind,*Chicago, University of Chicago Press.

Blanchard-Fields, John; C Cavanaugh, Fredda (2009), *Adult Development and Aging* (6th Ed.), Australia, Wadsworth/Cengage Learning.

Bryant, W (1993) *The Veiled Pulse of Time: Life Cycles and Destiny*, NY, Lindisfarne.

Fonda, J (2011) *Prime TimeLove, Health, Sex, Fitness, Friendship, Spirit; Making the most of all of your Life,*NY, Random House.

Fuller, A (2011) *Life: A Guide. What to expect in each seven-year stage*, Sydney, Finch.

Jung, Carl. *The Portable Jung* ed. Joseph Campbell, NY, Penguin Books.

Lievegoed, B (1985) *Man on the Threshold,*Stroud, Hawthorn Press.

O'Neil, G& O'Neil, G (1998) *The Human Life,*NY, Mercury Press.

Peterson, C (2010) *Looking Forward through the Lifespan: Developmental Psychology,*Sydney, Pearson.

Soesman (2009) *The Twelve Senses,* Stroud, Hawthorn Press.

Staley, B (1997) *Tapestries: Weaving Life's Journey*, Stroud, Hawthorn Press.

The art of growing old is the art of being regarded by the oncoming generations as a support and not as a stumbling-block.

—Andre Maurois, *An Art of Living*
http://www.notable-quotes.com/o/old_age_quotes.
html#AV6Plo0Si2ETC4RG.99

CHAPTER 12

Old Age: 70 -77 years
"Sharing more wisdom"

Introduction

The period of 70-77 years of age mirrors the period of 28 to 35 years of age and is influenced by the sun with its warmth and creative energy. If a person has passed into their 70s with good health, then it is likely they may experience a resurgence of creative energy and a sense of renewed life forces. During this time they may engaged in new creative activities, write their life story, attend painting classes or explore other gifts and ideas that they have always wanted to discover. O'Neil and O'Neil (1990. p.226) describe this transition forcefully:

> The healing presence and the warm, gentle glow– or the fiery enthusiasm for new beginnings– of those who have in this way reached their 80s is then a source of great inspiration for all.

This is the time when there is still the energy to spread one's wings, and if health is good– as it is increasingly these days– there is still time to travel, discover new things and people and continue with the active grand-parenting role providing kind, gentle and wise guidance to that generation. There is time to share their awe and wonder at the world and to make up for all the missed moments with your own children when you were running to a tight time schedule. My mother was a great blessing to my family during this age phase as she babysat my young babies and then cared for them so often when they were young children while I worked, or during holiday periods. The children developed great attachment to her, her home, the interesting activities and games they played together, her special treats and the time out with nanna. On her 90th birthday, my son gave his nanna a card, which read:

Happy birthday nanna and thanks nanna for helping me buy my first suit, my first car and all the special presents you bought me, all the games we

played and especially all the ice creams you bought me that I was not sup-
posed to have...

This is the time in which there is plenty of time to deepen your relationships with grandchildren, family, friends and with the meaningful parts
of the world around you. My mother and her sister were central to family
celebrations, gatherings, outings and all the core events that happened in our
family life.

Physical development

Seventy-two years is a significant signpost in human life and for many years
was regarded as the year marking the end of a human life. These days the
72-year barrier has been well and truly broken with life expectancy for men
rising to 84 and for women to 86 years. Effectively, we are facing a longevity
revolution with extra years of vitality and energy available for many people.
Fonda in *Prime Time* talks about this period as the "third act" and she defines
11 ingredients for successful ageing during this time which include not abus-
ing alcohol, not smoking, getting enough sleep, being physically active and
eating healthily. They also include continuous learning, a positive attitude,
reviewing and reflecting on life, loving and staying connected with friends
and family, giving of yourself to others and caring about the bigger picture of
your community, your nation, the planet so that you locate yourself within
the ongoing stream of life.

Fonda (2012,p.213) emphasizes in *Prime Time* that an ongoing sexually
satisfying lifestyle is a core part of the older years and cites studies showing
that a satisfying sexual relationship reduces the risk of heart disease, depression, migraine, arthritis, stress and boosts the immune system. Although sexual performance declines in older years, particularly among men, there are no
known age limits to sexual activity.

The ageing process does affect many parts of the body. The immune system declines with ageing so the need for greater dietary care is essential. There
are also declines in visual acuity, colour vision and depth perception with
a rise in the eye diseases of cataracts, glaucoma and macular degeneration.
Generally, there is an ongoing decline in the sense of hearing, smell, taste and
touch but a greater sensitivity to temperature changes and in particular cold
(Santrock, 2006).

Walking and balance are also affected with ageing but keeping fit and
following a regular exercise program has very significant impacts on prevent-
ing balance and walking difficulties and reversing declines that have already
occurred in the older years. My mother walked 10km a day until she had a

fall and broke her hip at 87, and when given a whole body bone scan had the bone density of a healthy 60 year old.

Clearly, ageing is not a uniform process, and hereditary as well as life-style choices and mental attitude can be very variable among the aged in this category.

Psychological: Cognitive development

As the brain of older adults shrinks, it adapts in a number of ways. Humans can grow new brain cells depending on environmental stimulation. Older brains also rewire themselves so they can solve problems but differently to younger brains. With ageing, the parts of the brain tend to integrate cognition and emotion and this facilitates reflection, insight and holistic thinking. Using both hemispheres improves cognitive functioning in the older years (Santrock, 2006, p.563). Using your brain for cognitive activities keeps it fit and healthy and acts as the best preventative to ageing and brain breakdown disease that occur in old age.

This is the ideal age at which to complete a life review, to write about your life in a critically reflective way that brings the pieces together and creates connectedness and insight around your journey through life to date. It can also be an opportunity for forgiveness, letting go and moving into a place where we can breathe deeply and be at peace with our own soul.

Psychological social: Emotional development

The 72-year Jupiter cycle provides the opportunity to bring new energy that captures the essence of one's life work in a new and vital away. It can be a time for pursing parts of one's vocation that have previously lain dormant. My mother resurrected her great passion for art that she had abandoned as an adult –consumed with her teaching career –and took up art classes with enthusiasim and vigour. She produced more than a hundred paintings over the next 16 years. The art classes also provided social connections with a group of senior people engaged in art work which inspired her work and gave her a cohort with which to share her artistic journey. Many seniors choose a creative activity like art to renew their social relationships and to engage in a satisfying activity.

The great psycho-emotional challenge of this period of ageing is to transform the senses from being focused physically and personally to spiritual and social focuses, so we can embrace others and remain connected to others. Our sense of touch flourishes if we continue to touch the garden, a pet, our grandchildren, through sewing, knitting and craftwork or playing music. Our sense of life even when we feel unwell is transformed by a loving act for a friend or a neighbour. My mother was the cake and biscuit maker in the street, carrying her treats to neighbours to cheer them up if she heard they were unwell. We retain our sense of movement by using our limbs through regular exercise, walking with friends, swimming or dancing. Our sense of balance is nurtured if we develop inner peace, contentment with that which is within us and not seeking a host of things to add to our lives. Our sense of smell weakens but our connection to the moral needs of the world through compassion in our thoughts or deeds can become enlivening. Through releasing our sense of taste for things and directing it towards a taste for beauty and goodness we nourish our soul. While the physical sense of warmth may diminish, we can cultivate a warm heart and radiate with unconditional love for family and children. As our sense of hearing declines, we can cultivate the inner silence, focused concentration and mindfulness more readily so we are less distracted and more able to be present. Our sense of thought is nurtured by deepening an open mind and cultivating the inner silence for which new insights can arise. Through our sense of ego– that is, the part that perceives the moral calibre of another human being– we can cultivate with ageing a greater tolerance, more kindness and less criticism (Staley, 2009). If we see the decline in the acuity of our outer senses as an opportunity to create and transform our inner senses, much wisdom is gained and we avoid becoming trapped in the negative thinking of ageing as a body breaking down. We begin to realise that it is a body in transformation for a more inward life, a recollecting of experience to bring back to the human spirit.

Spiritual development

As the senses decline, the space for the spirit to rise and come to the fore of human life is created. We can go slowly and notice the beauty of the small things in life and marvel at the mystery of so many things we take for granted as adults in a rush to achieve some task. It is often possible to contribute on a volunteer basis or embark on a part-time career at this age. There is wisdom to share without the distraction of promotions and career ambitions. Loneliness and aloneness are the great malaises of the ageing spirit, where the elderly retreat into themselves and slowly seem to fade away, first from their community, then their family and finally themselves. It is as though their spirit has packed its bags and left even before the physical body has died. The physical body seems to be a hollow shell and the eyes are dull. Without strong connections to family or friends, these people die alone or populate old age homes like scarecrows, bodies without spirit.

Developmental decisions

My daughter and her family live overseas and I have to make a 19-hour flight to visit them, which exhausts me. Is it still ok to be doing this at 75 years of age?

Family connections are very important to one's psycho-emotional health but these days the physical stresses of long-haul air travel can be very debilitating. Consider some alternative options like breaking the trip into legs and staying overnight along the journey. Flying business class with a sleeper if you can afford it or alternatively paying your daughter to come home to visit you. There is no one answer but it is a balance between the physical cost and the emotional benefits.

My mother lives alone five hours from the nearest family member, and since my father died stays home most of the time. She is losing weight, seems listless and is not motivated to do anything but watch TV. How can she be helped?

Clearly, grief and loss are critical problems for an aged person who loses a spouse. Support through grief and loss is essential. There are some counselling services that will do home visits, particularly if your mother is also feeling depressed. Of course, all of this depends on your mother wanting to reach out and accept some help along the way. It would be excellent if she would agree to Meals on Wheels so that she has nutritious meals provided for her. Finding a social group with an interest she shares is very important and many services will pick her up from home and drop her off at the end of the day. Staying alone and isolated is the least desirable situation for her. Every act that increases her contact with caring others and that supports her needs and her interests is health promoting. Of course, though, she may need some family member who she respects and loves to inspire her to start to undertake these activities and initially to organise them for her as many elderly feel powerless and overwhelmed, particularly after the death of a long-term loved spouse.

Conclusion

This phase of the life span confirms that ageing with its benefits and handicaps is an inescapable fact. Not all the plastic surgery or all the cruises can detract one from this knowledge in the 70s. There is still much energy to be harnessed for life, but the pace of life must slow down so that one's spirit gathers the inner resources and courage to stand strong in the face of the body's decline over the remaining years of life. It is a phase of preparation while the physical body is robust enough to make the essential transformations to a life that is more focused on the present moment and the slower rhythmic pace of the older years.

> What I feel I have come to understand is really simply this; none of us has any choice when it comes to getting old. It is above all else a fact. There are surely some pleasures left, but also plenty of tough challenges, often coming at a time when we feel least equipped to face them. Old age is about courage, it is about making the choice as to whether or not to be defeated by ageing or live out one's remaining years with style (Mary Sarton cited in Staley 1997, p.257).

SUMMARY

- I need to engage actively in my family and community life.
- I need to use my senses in ways that keep me in touch with the world within myself and the world around me.
- I need to be needed and volunteer work can keep me positively connected to the world.
- I need to drop the clutter of my physical life so I can concentrate on the essential emotional and spiritual connections in my life.
- I need to find a meaningful place for my spirit to connect with world.

REFERENCES

Fonda, J (2011) *PrimeTimeLove, Health, Sex, Fitness, Friendship, Spirit; Making the most of all of your Life,* NY, Random House.

Fuller, A (2011) *Life: A Guide. What to expect in each seven-year stage,* Sydney, Finch.

O'Neil, G& O'Neil, G (1998) *The Human Life,* NY, Mercury Press.

Santrock, J (2006) *Life Span Development,* NY, McGraw Hill.

Staley, B (1997) *Tapestries: Weaving Life's Journey,* Stroud, Hawthorn Press.

When you were born , you cried and the world rejoiced.
Live your life so that when you die, the world cries and you rejoice.

—White Elk

Older Age: 77-84 years onwards "Reviewing the life journey"

Introduction

As old people move through the retirement phase into old age, our health, vigour and quality of life depend a great deal on the aged person's experience of being connected to their family system. Aged persons who can maintain an active connection with their family and loved ones do much better in many areas of their lives than aged persons who are isolated in aged care facilities, visited only occasionally, if at all, by those who are meaningful to them. When my mother fell and broke her hip at 87 years, the hospital registrar informed me that there was a 75 per cent chance of recovery, including walking again, if she came home to live with her family and only a 35 per cent chance if she was relocated to an aged care facility after the surgery. The decision was made in my heart that she must have a chance to recover and walk again and so she came to spend the remainder of her life in my home with my two teenage children, Sam the Labrador and a troupe of day carers. She became the heart of our family system over the next five years and the whole house was organised around her needs and her carers. From living alone and depressed in a distant city, she became part of our family contributing to the laughter, humour, education and conversation, especially with her grandchildren, and within a year there were no signs of depression or lethargy. She was a great source of learning for my teenagers aged 13 and 16 who learned, in response to her needs, compassion and kindness. When she was ill and needed assistance at many inconvenient times of the night and day, the family rallied around to help. Nanna become lead character in many dramatic skits my daughter developed for her drama classes and she generously contributed to helping them buy their first car and their first ball clothes.

So often she reminded us that despite the grey hair, bent shoulders and the sound of her walker scrapping across the floor, that she was not old and she always carried in her handbag her life story she had written about her career as a teacher spanning more than 40 years. She would share this book with anyone who was willing – or unwilling – to listen and kept copies for distribution to those people who did not have time to listen to her rendition of it. It was her way of reminding everybody that she was a wise old woman with a wealth of achievements in her life. I remember when she was 90 years old, an audiologist once telling her that she had only 15 per cent hearing left in one ear and 35 per cent in the other ear. She quietly opened her handbag, took out a copy of her teaching career and handed it over to him with the comment: "Read this young man, I have done a great deal in my life and I can still hear enough to know that you need to read this to know what I am capable of... Hearing aids I don't need...I shall just flush them down the toilet." To the end of her life, even when the dementia crept in, she would have her carers read to her excerpts from her life career and she would sit quietly with a contented smile on her face. She had become a teacher against great odds, an Italian migrant, classified at age 17 as enemy alien number 72 during WWII. She attended a country high school and the state university despite requiring police passes daily to travel and threats from the local policeman that "we will never let people like you teach our children" (meaning Italian migrants). She had remarkable stamina, persistence and intelligence to be the first female Italian migrant in Western Australia to become a schoolteacher. She was very proud of her accomplishment, loved her career and taught for more than 40 years. At a time when my teenagers were preparing for the final year exams to enter university, she remained an inspirational icon in their lives, daily reminding them that education was a lifelong gift and opportunities should always be treasured.

Old people have so much to offer, particularly when they have harvested their life journey but the pace is so much slower. It is as though they are reflecting in a still forest pool, while the rest of us swirl around in the tumultuous seas. Often this discrepancy in pace makes communication difficult between the generations and for younger generations to erroneously believe that old people have little to offer. My teenage daughter Tara, who was always a night owl and stayed up to 2am on a regular basis, shared wonderful conversations in the wee quiet hours of the morning between one and 2am with her grandmother. The stillness of the starry night in the quiet countryside in which we lived seemed to connect them deeply in a rhythm of deep communication. In the last weeks of her life, when my mother lay dying in hospital it was her granddaughter Tara who insisted on sleeping next to her bed on a mattress on the floor, holding her hand.

Physical development

Old people and children are on opposite ends of the growth curve, the former declining physically, the latter growing into their physical strength. However, they both share a special interest in food, which is the primary way of connecting with the physical body in these age groups. Just as children are often fussy about food, tastes and textures, so too do old people become fussy about food, tastes and textures. When my mother, who had always eaten very healthily and insisted we did as children, began to buck the healthy food eating rules, I failed to understand. I insisted she eat her greens, particularly her broccoli and was horrified that my health-food conscious mother was rejecting this good food with comments like disgusting and yucky. After all, I was the first child in the whole school to have wholemeal bread and not to be allowed lollies because they were bad for you. My cakes never had icing on the top because sugar "just fed the worms, made your teeth rot, made you fat and caused diabetes". It was all very clear to me. I failed to understand why my mother tried to bribe the carers into buying her regular supplies of chocolate, hid lollies in her handbag and munched on them before meals, all serious travesties of the healthy eating rules under which I had been brought up and to which I still adhered. If I had studied my aged life span development better, I would have had more compassion and not scolded her when she was caught eating sugar before meals. When I commented one day half-jokingly to my mother: "My mother would never approve of eating sweets before meals" she just grinned and said: "But they taste so much better before meals." My daughter understood. As a young adolescent she understood so well her grandmother that she would leave little chocolate frogs near her bed-side table at night, so when her nanna woke she could have her special treat before breakfast.

This sensitivity to and reactiveness to some food is a particular way of connecting with the world and a way of old people staying alive and well. I remember a very experienced age carer who was very wise in managing old people, always gently but skilfully. When I wept on his shoulder one day saying that I feared my mother was going to die because during her two-month recuperation after her hip surgery she repeatedly said she was going to die, he replied kindly: "Dear, anybody who eats as much food as your mother and with as much enthusiasm and appetite five times a day has no intention of dying."

In terms of body appearance, a number of characteristics emerge in this late old age period. This includes significant weight decline as muscle tissue now wastes away and fat gets used up faster than normal. There is bone tissue loss continuing at a significant rate particularly for women, of whom 66 per cent have osteoporosis. Chronic disease accelerates and the quantity of medications rise to extraordinary heights with many old people over 80 years taking at least 10 different prescribed medications per day. Skin becomes increasingly thin, and pre-occupation with wound care and management are of central concern with those over 80 years, particularly following falls or injuries of any type as the recovery and healing time is very much longer than in earlier stages of the life span.

The most common chronic disease among this aged group is arthritis, followed by high blood pressure. Currently, there is a rapid increase in dementia and Alzheimer's in the aged population, particularly those over 80 years old.

Psychological: Cognitive development

There is still time to think differently, to analyse the rules and to delight in breaking them, either consciously or half consciously. An old person's memory starts to fade and the past starts to mingle with the present (Staley, 2009, p.278). Often, the aged may become confused as many of their friends and relatives have now passed on. It is as though the boundaries between the living and the dead become thinner.

The old aged person is being released from the business of life and its demands. This is often expressed mentally as becoming less focused, less concerned with the day-to-day details of life, and living more and more in a world of their own, often with a dream-like look upon their countenance as though they are in some place far away. I remember my mother would often gaze out at the rolling hills around my home and tell me this was where she grew up and this must be her childhood home. While the geography was similar, the home was different but in her mind, these merged, especially as the dementia took a grip of her mind in her ninetieth year. Some days I was her mother, others, her sister and occasionally her daughter...it did not seem to matter to her which one. They were all people who cared for her in her life and as she moved closer to her death at 91 years, the merging of her close caring family seemed quite satisfactory for her.

Psychological social: Emotional development

Healthy psychological development in the aged is characterised by positive thinking and a focus on the emotional life, particularly with meaningful emotional connections of spouses and family members. In the best development, both men and women develop more fluency with their emotional lives in old age and more sensitivity to emotions, particularly negative emotions. Those aged persons who engage in social activities outside of the home report higher levels of happiness than those who remain isolated in their own home and generally have fewer doctors' visits than those persons who remain socially isolated. There are increasing numbers of social groups catering for aged persons and providing positive interactive opportunities funded by local, state and federal governments in Australia. My mother, while initially resisting joining groups of old people (because she was not old), was cajoled into an Italian group and an activities group. Twice a week until she died at 91 years she enjoyed her outings to her social groups. Every other day she would ask carers to take her for drives, to enjoy a morning or afternoon tea away from home, so that her life had a structure and a rhythm around food and social activities. The depression she had suffered while living alone in the city disappeared within 12 months and never returned.

When an ageing person does not grasp the freedom given by these years and clings to the false security of the known and the predictable, they coalesce into the past. They then fear the future and the present is full of regrets about the past. They can readily become pessimistic, critical, cold and detached from life around them. This is a retreat towards death rather than an embrace of the life they still have. Fuller (2012, p.177) describes the important challenge of this phase as:

> Gathering together the threads of your life, sifting the trivial from the essential and seeing a connection between yourself and the ongoing stream of human and natural existence is the key to freedom. People who gain this key gain the gift of being themselves. Aspiration and envy wash away, leaving a sense of being precisely who you are.

Spiritual development

All of this period is dominated by Saturn which governs the life force from 56 years onward demanding that everything non-essential to the spirit is gradually discarded. Material possessions become less and less important and the older person is pressured by Saturn to gather up the fruits of their biography, discard the non-essential material and create a space for the resurrection of the spirit as it prepares to return to the spiritual world from which it came (Lieviegoed, 1985, p.103). It is essential the old person has a peaceful image of dying and their fears are assuaged. Unfinished business is a great burden on the ageing person's spirit and every opportunity should be given to tie up the ends of such business so the aged person's spirit feels unencumbered and free to take flight at the appropriate time. My mother did not belong to the counselling generation but all the unfinished traumas of her life, her mother's violent death that she witnessed at seven years of age, the war trauma, all surfaced in family conversations repeatedly until she was at peace with them. They then disappeared quietly out of her mind and heart and a new peace came upon her.

In Australia, 85 per cent of people claim some sense of a spiritual or non-material experience or belief, while in the US the figure is 90 per cent. There is an increase in spiritual activities as people age. Spiritual beliefs and practices help aged individuals with a fear of death and pain, and may give them confidence to move through the dying process with calm and hope (Lavretsky, 2010, p.1). It may also help relatives and loved ones to better deal with the dying of their loved one and with the ensuing grief and loss. My mother loved the rosary and was devoted to Mary throughout her life, so in the last week of her life in hospital I made certain there were pictures of Mary in her room and I would recite the rosary with her, or for her when she was too weak to recite it herself. Although it was over 40 years since I had recited a rosary, I found strength and comfort in the words of the Hail Mary, which I had never really considered before in my life. I also found comfort in the rhythm of the recitation and at the end of each rosary felt more able to peacefully sit with my dying mother and support her needs. The palliative care unit conducted a profoundly moving spiritual but non-sectarian service for all persons who had lost family in that past six months and the service was very well attended and deeply appreciated by all there.

In terms of spiritual development, it is common as we move into old age a more universal spirituality develops, which is connectedness with the power of the universe and fellowship with other humans regardless of their faith or religious tradition. There is a movement in healthy ageing towards an embracing spirituality which is no longer ideologically driven but which is more heartfelt. Religious activity is also associated with decline in depression and suicide among the aged (Lavretsky, 2010).

Developmental decisions

I am in a great deal of pain and the prescribed medication is not helping me. I feel suicidal at times. What can I do?

Firstly, have a review of your medication and get a second opinion on what prescribed medication is being given to you and in what doses. Find a pain management clinic near you that helps one manage chronic pain. It may be worth trying out alternative types of pain management in the complementary medicine field. There are a range of pain management processes in acupuncture, acupressure, homeopathy, herbalism, Chinese medicine, naturopathy, Reiki, Johrei just to name just a few. Dr Kabat Zinn in his very influential book, *Full Catastrophe Living*, has identified a number of breathing techniques that assist in reducing pain and it is worth buying a copy of this book if you are interested in learning to manage your pain and try out some of the exercises. Working in counselling to learn to transform negative into positive thoughts to manage your pain may also be of assistance.

I have lost my spouse of 55 years and feel like I have died too. How is it possible to move on from this at my age?

Grief and loss is always a long healing process and crying from time to time is normal and healthy. If possible, avoid anti-depressants as these dumb you down. They tend to flat line all your feelings– the good ones as well as the grief– so life loses its human quality. Instead, remain connected with people and things you love. If you love the ocean, go and sit on the sand and cry there and let the water take your grief out to sea. Cry on a family member or friend's shoulder and share great memories about the loved one you have lost. Create icons to honour the person you have lost in any creative way that appeals to you. Plant a tree, plant a rose garden, write a poem, a song, make a collage in a scrapbook, create a photo gallery, paint a picture...the more you do with your hands to honour the life of the person you have loved, the easier the transition. Remember, repressing your feelings does not help while expressing them in creative ways does. Join a group of seniors who have also lost spouses or a bereavement support group. Keep connected to the things you love and enlarge your connections with people. These help the slow and painful recovery, which usually will take about 12 months just to feel you are over the bulk of it and probably another year to feel fully yourself again. The life body, or etheric body as it is known in this model, has a two-year healing cycle after serious grief and loss because it literally tears us apart when a loved one dies. It is also helpful to give away their possessions so that one is not reminded daily of their absence and to rearrange the living space so that it is a bit different. Many people feel that by writing letters or communicating with their loved one from time to time in their mind is also helpful, or saying prayers for them, depending on one's sense of the spiritual world. The following websites have helpful pointers to services that can support one through grief and loss. www.dhhs.tas.gov.au/palliative-care/patients/bereavementwww.grief.org.au/grief_and_bereavement_support

I do not want to be kept alive artificially when I am very ill. What can I do to ensure that these wishes are followed out?

Today it has become essential that you complete a document called a living will or a medical will. This enables you to state your preferences for medical treatment in a range of situations – keeping you alive using artificial nutrition and hydration in the short term and in the long term may not be desired if one could remain in a persistent vegetative state. One would also state one's wishes in relation to resuscitation, use of antibiotics in potentially terminal illness and the use of morphine and other opiates as the painkillers of non-choice or choice. All of these complications in health have very different implications for a young person compared to a person at 90 years of age who is frail and suffering. There are also documents that enable you to give the power of medical decision making to a friend or relative but the disadvantage of these is that they must make some very difficult life and death decisions. For example, at 91 my mother had a serious stroke that left her almost totally paralysed. In the next three weeks, despite attempts at eating, she began inhaling food into her lungs and developed pneumonia. She was distraught because she could no longer move– particularly walk – or eat properly. There was no hope of recovery of either of these capacities. I made the decision not to give her antibiotics but to allow her to die peacefully from pneumonia rather than keep her alive in a vegetative state on drips artificially feeding her. It was a painful decision but I believe the most humane, compassionate and respectful of her wish not to have invasive medical treatments but to be allowed to die peacefully and with dignity. One example of an advanced-care directive can be obtained at (http://www.hov.org/living-will-health-care-decisions).

Conclusion

This is a profound period of the life span. At 84 years, we complete four 21-year cycles. We are spiralling closer to the energy of the sun. Previously, it was experienced as the midlife crisis but at 84 years we are free to ascend to the light, released from the earthly burdens and cares of the early phase of the life span. After 84 years, we can live in a period of extended grace with the opportunity to flow with the rhythms of life and of nature until we return to the light from whence we came. This phase is so dependent on our mental emotional attitude...if we remain positive and strong in our minds, the decay of the body remains separate from the vitalisation of our spirit, now wise with the learning of a lifetime.

> People grow old only by deserting their ideals. Years may wrinkle the skin, but to give up interest wrinkles the soul... You are as young as your faith, as old as your doubt, as young as your self-confidence, as old as your fear, as young as your hope, as old as your despair. In the central place of every heart there is a recording chamber, so long as it receives messages of beauty, hope, cheer and courage, so long are you young. When...your heart is covered with the snows of pessimism and the ice of cynicism, then and only then are you grown old– and then indeed, as the ballad says, you just fade away (Staley, 1997, p.269).

The choice is not to fade away but to become a bright ray of light for younger generations holding a warm and soft glow in which peace and contentment are manifest.

SUMMARY

- I need to move forward and pursue my creativity in more inward ways.
- I need to appreciate the freedom that comes for my spirit with ageing and the release from physical responsibilities and see it as a doorway of new opportunities.
- I can become fussy about my food again and eat what I like.
- I can wear the colour purple as much as I like.
- I must remain connected to family and those I love.
- I must continue to have a social life that is full and rewarding that keeps my heart full and happy.
- I must connect to the rhythms of nature and maintain my own life rhythms so that there is flow in my daily activities.
- I need an advance directive for medical treatment so I am treated the way I want to be when I am ill.
- I accept the inevitability of death but celebrate life and live in the present moment.

REFERENCES

Fonda, J (2012) *Prime Time*, Vermillion, London.

Friedan, B (1994) *The Fountain of Age*, London, Vintage.

Fuller, A (2011) *Life: A Guide. What to expect in each seven-year stage*, Sydney, Finch

Kabat Zinn (2006) *Full Catastrophe Living: How to cope with stress, pain and illness using mindfulness meditation*, London, Piatkus.

Lavretsky, H (2010) Spirituality and Aging in *Aging Health*, 2010: 6(6): 749-769.

Lievegoed, B (1985) *Man on the Threshold*, Stroud, Hawthorn Press.

O'Neil, G& O'Neil, G (1998) *The Human Life*,NY, M ercury Press.

Peterson, C (2010) *Looking Forward through the Lifespan: Developmental Psychology*, Sydney, Pearson.

Staley, B (1997) *Tapestries: Weaving Life's Journey*, Stroud, Hawthorn Press.

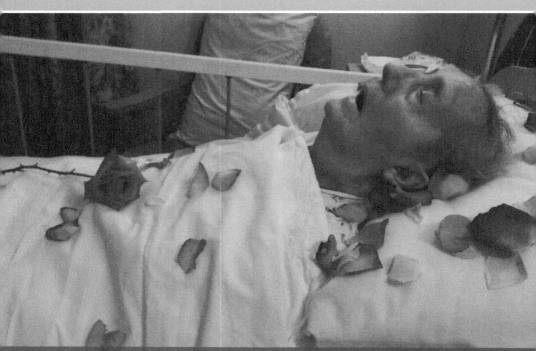

"When I stand before God at the end of my life, I would hope that I would not have a single bit of talent left, and could say, 'I used everything you gave me.'"
—Erma Bombeck

CHAPTER 14

Death and Life after Life: where to from here? "Death and dying"

Introduction

Death is the destination for everything physical and so death comes to us all. But as Einstein reminded us, energy is neither created nor destroyed but transformed from one form to another, and so it is that our physical body returns to the elements of earth and the etheric or life force to the elements of air, water and light from which it came. As the breath carrying the spirit of the person moves higher and higher up the body and finally leaves through a shuddering gasp, then the spirit or "I" disengages from the physical body and returns to the sun, the light from whence it came. This is an important transition process for the spirit bearing the accumulated wisdom and suffering of the life. All religious traditions document what cautions are to be taken to facilitate the movement of the spirit back to a place of light. Although the details vary, the intention remains the same which is to support a peaceful dying process and a return to a spiritual world. The preparation for dying is letting go, and letting go with peace long before the actual moment of death. This is why life review is an important process to undertake with an aged person so they can integrate their life experiences into a meaningful whole. Also, there is much to be said for the letting go of material possessions which clutter the mind and life of the ageing person. I remember an aged person re-wrapping all the possessions in their house that had been given as gifts to them and posting them back to their senders with a card thanking them for the gift of these items but that they were no longer needed. The aged person then retired to a village where she decided to spend her time in volunteer work and inner prayer.

One's physical needs are less and less, and one has the time and space to become well acquainted with oneself. Fear of death too often arises from avoidance of understanding the inner spirit of ourselves.

Perhaps the deepest reason why we are afraid of death is because we do not know who we are. We believe in a personal, unique and separate identity – but if we dare to examine it, we find that this identity depends entirely on an endless collection of things to prop it up; our name, our "biography", our partners, family, home, job, friends, credit cards… It is on their fragile and transient support that we rely for our security. So when they are all taken away, will we have any idea of who we really are? Without our familiar props, we are faced with just ourselves, a person we do not know, an unnerving stranger with whom we have been living all the time but we never really wanted to meet. Isn't that why we have tried to fill every moment of time with noise and activity, however boring or trivial, to ensure that we are never left in silence with this stranger on our own?" http://www.goodreads.com/author/quotes/60281.Sogyal_Rinpoche

The dying process needs to be completed with equanimity for the dying person so that they can easily collect themselves for their onward journey that is so brilliantly described in *The Tibetan Book of the Dead:*

> Remember the clear light, the pure, clear, white light from which everything in the universe comes, to which everything in the universe returns; the original nature of your own mind. The natural state of the universe unmanifest. Let go into the clear light. Trust it, merge with it. It is your home. (http://realizedone.com/tibetan-book-of-the-dead/)

I have been with a dying person and had the privilege to watch this process of the person slowly gathering their consciousness to leave their body and move into the immaterial realms of light. It can be difficult to complete this peaceful transition if the person is suffering from some disease, such as some types of cancer given some types of treatments. Other illnesses, such as pneumonia, while difficult for onlookers are comparatively painless for the dying person and the dying process can be completed more easily. As morphine based painkillers alter the mind consciousness, those persons committed to conscious dying will do their best to avoid these and seek other alternatives for the management of pain. There are long traditions of using natural products for pain relief and some are documented in this website (http://www.mnwelldir.org/docs/therapies/pain.htm). Clearly the dying person's medical directive can assist relatives make the difficult decisions when the dying person is no longer conscious.

However, it is more important a person dies being accompanied and with the sense of being loved rather than alone. It was Mother Teresa who brought to our attention the great human need to die with love and not alone, to die in the presence of another human being who cares for us. She reminded us that dying of lack of love is a disease:

The greatest disease in the West today is not TB or leprosy; it is being unwanted, unloved and uncared for. We can cure physical diseases with medicine but the only cure for loneliness, despair and hopelessness is love. There are many in the world who are dying for a piece of bread but there are many more dying for a little love. The poverty in the West is a different kind of poverty – it is not only a poverty of loneliness but also of spirituality. There's a hunger for love, as there is a hunger for God.

My mother died slowly over seven days from pneumonia and she gave the great gift to family and relatives of dying peacefully and surrounded by our love. During the days and nights of her dying there were moments of intense gratitude for her life but there were also moments when I wanted her to die faster. I believed it was because I wanted her suffering to end quickly but the reality was that she was not suffering…she was peacefully slipping away. It was my suffering of losing her that was intolerable at moments, my anguish of the letting go process that the face of death demands. It is hard to be with the dying and face your ultimate powerlessness to fix things, to make things better. I admired my friend who could peacefully hold my mother's hand while I sat in the room hoping the pieces of my breaking heart would not shatter around her room that we had so carefully covered in rose petals, her favourite flower. My daughter's grief was palpable and she had twice before called my mother back to life after near-death experiences. We had to leave for just a quick evening meal at the end of the day and my mother chose this time to leave. She died peacefully with my composed friend who guided her through the final dying process.

The dying process is often so complicated by the grief of the family observers that it can make it difficult for the person trying to pass through to the light realms to actually depart. So often nursing staff report that the person slipped away in the 10 minutes the relatives went to get a cup of tea, to eat something or just went to the toilet. When my father visited me about three days after his death I asked him why he died before I could get to the hospital to see him. He simply replied: "I loved you too much to be able to say goodbye to you and my body was worn out. I needed to leave and it was easiest if you were not there."

The dying process is inextricably complicated by the grieving process of those left behind and the grieving journey only begins with the death of the loved one. In our loss, we need to deeply understand Frye's thoughts:

Do not stand at my grave and weep;
I am not there, I do not sleep
I am a thousand winds that blow
I am the sunlight on reapered grain

I am the gentle autumn rain.
When you awaken in the morning's hush
I am the swift uplifting rush
Of quiet birds in circled flight
I am the soft stars that shine at night
Do not stand at my grave and cry
I am not here
I did not die.

(Cited in Fuller, 2011, p.177)

However, the reality for the etheric bodies of the bereaved is that the energetic resonance of the deceased person is still vibrating within them. In the case of close family members it takes a minimum of one year to feel one is over the gap in one's soul left by their death, and a second year to really start to feel whole and complete in oneself again. I thought I understood deep grief. I had lost my father, and for several weeks I lost track of day or night or eating or sleeping times. I remember the months of the recurrent guilt of "did I do enough for him". In addition, the final letting go came as my son was born nine months later, and was given his name. However, unlike my father, my mother had lived with me for five years. I was her carer and I was unprepared for the extent of grief that would follow. Physically and etherically the daily rhythms of my life changed radically. The emotional resonance of her presence caused me to dissolve into tears at the slightest memory of her and I felt quite out of control. I cried in banks, in lawyers' offices, at the florist, at the sight of anything from food to flowers to pictures that my mother loved. I questioned repeatedly; could I have increased her life by more vitamins, more minerals, another type of food...all part of the circuit of grief. Fortunately, I had good friends who helped me share the stages of grief and loss and I understood the importance of doing a ritual to honour the lost one. With my daughter, we created a scrapbook collage of my mother's life and designed a memorial headstone, which we knew honoured my mother's gifts. Remembering the lost one through ritual is core to all cultures and the loss of religious tradition in our secular society often leaves the bereaved person without a commemorative ritual or process. It is essential to design one so that the bereaved person or family may continue to release their grief.

Kubler Ross's stages (Santrock, 2006, p.644) that affect the dying person of denial, anger, bargaining for more time, depression and acceptance of death may not be typical of the very old who often make comments like, "I'm waiting for God to come and get me", "I'm ready to go now", "I wonder if I've been forgotten" often in the most accepting tone of voice and with equanimity. This is common in the ages of 87 to 90-plus and increases with age. My 91-year-old mother who was in good health had quite peacefully announced a couple of months before her final stroke that she was ready to go now and that she felt she had done her work here. Rather, it was myself and my daughter who went through Kubler Ross's stages. Firstly, denying that the severe crippling stroke could not be reversed at 91 years of age and insisting on physio for her. The anger at myself that I should not have left her in respite while I worked away and anger at the respite facility for not having recognised the first minor stroke. We did not bargain or go into depression but finally we had to admit that the end was approaching as she could no longer swallow food without it going into her lungs and she had developed pneumonia. Staley (1997,p.295) notes that with the loss of a loved one we go through the same stage ourselves as if it were us that were dying and that losing a parent is like losing part of ourselves. Giving a loved one, especially when aged and with great physical disability, permission to die contributes towards creating a space for them of peace and gratitude for their life. This space is important for both the dying person and the loved ones. It releases us all from suffering.

Life after life

After we die, religious organisations have proposed a journey to different realms variously called nirvana, heaven, the heavenly realms, the pure land, the bliss realms, zion, paradise, city of God. Of these states, we cannot know experientially. However, we can share the experiences of people who have died and come back against medical predictions to live again in their physical body and to further pursue their lives. These experiences are described as near-death experiences and defined by Sutherland (1992, p.3) as follows:

> The near death experience (NDE) is said to occur when a person is close to death (or in many cases clinically dead) and yet is resuscitated or somehow survives to recount an intense, profoundly meaningful experience.

Many persons have described their experiences of what happened after death and these have been well documented by Moody (1986). The common themes experienced by many hundreds of persons are collectively represented in the following description. Initially, there is the experience of hearing themselves pronounced dead, or following great physical distress, realising they are leaving their body. There is often a strange noise – uncomfortable or ringing– while the persons feel themselves to be moving very rapidly through a long, dark tunnel. After this journey, the person experiences themselves as outside of this body and often looking down on their body and the people who are concerned about them. The person realises they now have a lighter body, and as they look around they become aware of loving deceased relatives who have come to meet them and a bright light which seems to represent a being of light which is variously named according to their religious tradition. The being greets him or her with great love and asks them questions about their life following a panoramic flashback of their life presented by the being. They are helped to gain insight into their life during the life review process. At some time in the experience the person approaches a barrier between this world and another world and they are given the choice of whether to cross the barrier to the next world or to return to this world. During this experience, people report being overwhelmed with joy, love and peace beyond what they have known on Earth but they choose to return to the Earth because of love for family members or something they have left unfinished.

Sutherland (1992,p.3) notes that 5-10 percent of the population in America, claim to have had such an experience. She summarises it as follows:

> The near death episode itself is typically characterised by a feeling of peace, an out of the body experience, the sensation of travelling very quickly through a dark tunnel, generally towards a light, an encounter with the spirits of deceased relatives or friends or a being of light, an instantaneous life-review, and for some, entrance into a world of light.

The after-effects of near-death experiences are profound, and many describe it as a sort of "shock" returning to the world with a whole new world view. Essentially, their old world view has been shattered and they return to the same world but with a more expansive and profound world view that makes many of the day-to-day happenings seem trivial, petty or irrelevant. Sutherland (1996) notes that many people undergo a radical transformation in so far as they have a new attitude to life that is more positive, accepting and loving, and that they begin new careers that are more service orientated. They change relationships with others so that they are more focused and present to authentic relationships. Many report their lives are deepened by the experience and they now approach life with a more reflective attitude and one that is no longer focused purely on material gain. Significantly, persons who have had a near-death experience find that upon their return they are more accepting of themselves and more loving towards humanity in general. Their positivity increases in many respects and there is a longing for great knowledge, beyond what was previously understood by the person. It can be deduced that as the person who has had the near-death experience changes, so to do those intimately connected with them as they accommodate the changes in their loved one.

West (1998, p.395) summarises the core characteristics of the near-death experience as follows:

1. Leaving the body, travelling and returning to the body.
2. Experiencing infinity and no boundaries with a surrender to and/or merging with a higher power.
3. Experiencing divine refuge and/or homecoming with extraordinary feelings of love, acceptance, peace and joy.
4. Experiencing absolute truth and divine knowledge.
5. Perceiving the experience as ineffable.
6. Perceiving the experience as a personal message.
7. Perceiving the experiences as transformational.

Of course, individuals emphasize different aspects of the experience of the other realms but universally there is the feeling that this has been a profound experience with life changing effects on their world views and values, and the encounter with these other realms is positive and life affirming. It is not to be feared but rather something that can be experienced as loving, warm, welcoming and accepting. No accounts report hell states or other punishing structures. Near-death experience research demonstrates that the future after this incarnation is positive, affirming, non-judgmental and transformative, embracing the person with love, warmth and understanding while simultaneously providing them with new knowledge and purpose. Greyson, cited in Sutherland (1998, p.32), summarises near-death experiences well as "seed experiences and it is only by studying the fruits that eventually grow from those seeds that we can understand their full meaning". I would add that these seeds also offer all of us a glimpse into the ongoing journey of life after life.

Conclusion

The life-span journey has come full cycle, taking the person back to the light from whence they came in an expanding embrace from the world of light, and the welcome home appears warm, encouraging and supportive of joy, peace and happiness. Fear and judgment are banished in the face of unconditional love and the expansion of one's insight and knowledge through the ultimate life-review process as one reflects from the spiritual world on the wisdom one has acquired during one's life. One has completed one's journey through all the planetary influences to arrive back to the realms of the light, ultimately represented by the sun.

The cycle of this life is completed and one realises at the deepest level the life span is not linear but cyclical.

SUMMARY

- I need to remember that all things are impermanent and everything is in flux and change, including my body and my life.

- I need to live in the present moment and enjoy life fully. I do not know how many moments I have left to live.

- I need to connect to the cycles of life, my children and grandchildren, the seasons, the rhythms of my age.

- I need to celebrate the positives in life and avoid focusing on the negatives: I need to remember the cup is half full not half empty.

- I need to express gratitude regularly for the small, medium and large things in my life because gratitude is the most health promoting emotion for the heart.

- When I die I need to look upwards and towards the light.

- When I die I will complete my life review with wisdom and let go of negativity of any sort.

REFERENCES

Fuller, A (2011) *Life: A Guide. What to expect in each seven-year stage,* Sydney, Finch.

Moody, R (1986) *Life after Life,* NY, Bantam.

Mother Teresa (1995) *A Simple Path: Mother Teresa,* NY, Ballantine.

Santrock, J (2006) *Life Span Development,* NY, McGraw Hill.

Staley, B (1997) *Tapestries: Weaving Life's Journey,* Stroud, Hawthorn Press.

Sutherland, C (1996) *Transformed by the Light: Life after near-death experiences,* Sydney, Bantam.

Sambhava, Padma trans. Robert Thurman (2006) *The Tibetan Book of the Dead,*NY, Viking.

West, T (1998)"On the Encounter with a Divine Presence during a near death Experience"in *Phenomenological Inquiry in Psychology:* edit Valle, R, NY, Plenum Press, pp.387-406.

Lightning Source UK Ltd.
Milton Keynes UK
UKOW07f1141210615
253863UK00009B/44/P

9 780980 404432